C.A.R.N. CRITICAL CONVERSATIONS

BOOK ONE
THE ROLE OF SELF IN ACTION RESEARCH

C.A.R.N. Critical Conversations

Series Editors: Tony Ghaye, Jean McNiff
             and Peter Wakefield

C.A.R.N. CRITICAL CONVERSATIONS

BOOK ONE
THE ROLE OF SELF IN ACTION RESEARCH

Edited by
Tony Ghaye and Peter Wakefield

Hyde Publications

© Tony Ghaye and Peter Wakefield
and the authors of individual papers.

All rights reserved. No reproduction, copy or transmission of any part of this work may be made without written permission from the publisher.

First edition 1993

Published by Hyde Publications
57, Exeter Road, Bournemouth,
Dorset. BH5 2AF

ISBN 1-874154-02-3

Typeset, Printed and Bound by
Bourne Press Limited, Bournemouth

CONTENTS

	Page
Acknowledgements	viii
Foreword	ix
Introducing the Editors	xiii

Conversation One: Kevin Eames and Nick Clay 1
A Dialectical Form of Action Research-
Based Educational Knowledge:
A Teacher-Researcher's View
    Kevin Eames 2

What I would like to discuss with you
    Nick Clay 19

And in reply,
    Kevin Eames 23

Conversation Two: Alice Otto and Teresa Lehane 27
Graduate Medical Education: Research's
Outer Limits
    Alice Otto 28

What I would like to discuss with you
    Teresa Lehane 41

And in reply,
    Alice Otto 44

Conversation Three: Colin Henry and Bridget Somekh 47
McDonald's, Republicanism and Botham's
Early Departure: Democratic Education
for a Change
    Colin Henry.. 48

What I would like to discuss with you
    Bridget Somekh 73

And in reply,
    Colin Henry.. 79

Conversation Four:	Jill Burton, Peter Mickan and Peter Scrimshaw	83
	Managing Action Research Jill Burton and Peter Mickan	84
	What I would like to discuss with you Peter Scrimshaw	98
	And in reply, Jill Burton and Peter Mickan	102
Conversation Five:	Margot Ely and Jack Whitehead	105
	Write On: Stories About Telling It Margot Ely	106
	What I would like to discuss with you Jack Whitehead	129
	And in reply, Margot Ely.	133
Bibliography		139
Index		145

DEDICATION

Daphne, Beverley, Alistair & Jackie
" .... you are the wind beneath my wings."

To all those who are committed to improving the quality of education.

ACKNOWLEDGEMENTS

'Without dialogue there is no communication and without communication there can be no true education.'

[Freire, P., 1990, The Pedagogy of
the Oppressed, p. 65]

This is an opportunity to express our indebtedness. We gladly acknowledge it.

To begin with we wish to acknowledge colleagues from the Worcester Action Research Group who worked so hard during the C.A.R.N. Conference 1992, supported us, nourished us with their ideas and conversations and who have, through their own action research work, improved the quality of education in their own workplaces. Long may it continue. We thank:

Barbara Allen, Lynn Biggs, Maggie Blackman, Jane Bunting, Peter Burns, Sue Burrows, Brian Clarke, Jim Cobbett, Liz Dancey, Doug Dennis, Lynda Fotheringham, Jessie Garner, Chris Garner, Jeanette Gosling, Mary Griffin, Stephen Hewitt, Joan Holford, Ann Hunt, Peter Huntingdon, Elaine Josephson, Deidre Leeming, Debbie Mitchell, Kerry Newman, Steve Phillipson, Chris Purser, Kay Raees-Danai, Ruth Reeves, Neville Sheldrick, Nanette Smith, Reg Thomas, Jeanette Vincent, Sally Wakeham and Maggie Walker ... and particularly Margaret Comerford for her unstinting secretarial and administrative support.

We also acknowledge the encouragement we have received from Bridget Somekh and the C.A.R.N. Steering Group. Thanks also to all the contributors who have entered into the spirit of critical conversations.

Special thanks go to Jean McNiff, Alan Hyde and Hyde Publications without whose energy, vision and commitment the notion of a trilogy of C.A.R.N. Critical Conversations would have remained as just another good idea.

FOREWORD

Autumn, Worcester, and a meeting of a group of action researchers.

Jean   I wonder what kind of books on action research we would like to see on the shelf in two years' time?

Peter   Books with descriptions and explanations of the work of practitioners. Work that they are producing for their own educational development.

Kerry   Action research books that are lively, enjoyable, informative and extending.

Kay   Books with cases that enable me to understand what educational improvement looks and feels like.

Tony   Texts that invite me to engage with the action researcher's lived experiences.

Jean   Books where the text is accessible, authentic and dialogical.

C.A.R.N. Critical Conversations is a trilogy of books, drawn in part from the 1991 and 1992 C.A.R.N. International Conferences. Book One is called *The Role of Self in Action Research*. Book Two is entitled *Dimensions of Action Research: People, Practice and Power*. Book Three focuses on the theme *Creating Cultures for Improvement: Dialogue, Decisions and Dilemmas*.

The three books aim to encompass the following six qualities:

◆ **Participatory:** The books are an attempt to create an interactive and co-operative activity between writer and reviewer.

◆ **Grounded:** The action research accounts are undertaken in particular workplaces and relate to particular people and concerns.

◆ **Critical:** The format encourages the action researcher to reflect critically on her or his work and the nature of the account with added stimulus from the reviewer.

◆ **Democratic:** Writers and reviewers have equal rights in constructing the conversation. First there is the presentation of an account of some action research, then the review, and then a response to the review.

♦ **Affective:** The books reflect a range of emotions. For example, those associated with anxiety, exhilaration, puzzlement, enlightenment, pain and understanding.

♦ **Conversational:** The basic format of the books is a conversation between action researchers. It is a conversation about the issues and concerns that arise from their work and their understanding of it. The conversational form allows two people to express a personal point of view and to respond to each other and to the action research being presented. Action research presented in a conversational form is educational, professional and legitimate. These conversations represent something of the identities of those engaged in them. They convey a sense of self, a sense of relationship with another and a sense of commitment to understand self, others, and the context in which professional practice takes place.

Taken together the trilogy of C.A.R.N. Critical Conversations represents 'living' and developing conversations of:

♦ **Possibility:** They reflect not only what was thought and done, but what might have been, that 'which is not yet'. In this sense they are reflective.

♦ **Hope:** They describe and explain how action researchers have tried to bring about relevant, appropriate and meaningful educational improvement in a variety of workplaces.

♦ **Confrontation:** The action researcher's work should never be celebrated uncritically. In these books the writer is confronted with her or his own enquiry, and invited critically to reflect upon it with the help of the reviewer's questions and observations.

♦ **Liberation:** Each account in the trilogy is grounded in the action researcher's own life described and explained in her or his own words. The educational knowledge generated is something that the contributors to the books have created themselves in conditions of mutuality and respect.

C.A.R.N. CRITICAL CONVERSATIONS: BOOK ONE

We have called Book One *The Role of Self in Action Research.* Action research is not a value free activity. Quality action research is motivated by those who act with commitment and with a value-laden vision of a better world. These action researchers work purposefully and ethically towards realising that vision. Central to this enterprise is the notion of self. For example, there is the complex relationship between our understanding of self, self in relation to improvements in our own professional activity and the structures in which our actions take place. Then there is the action researcher's relationship with other 'selves', the learning from others, the critical friendships and the collective responsibility that is felt for realising educational values and priorities.

This is a book of personal thoughts and deeds, possibilities and hopes, confrontations with practice, and an authentic engagement by the contributors to explore and question examples of action research. Through a conversational form we hope that the book enables the writers, reviewers and readers of it to improve aspects of the way they see themselves and improve their abilities to become critical examiners of their own work and workplaces.

A feature of each of the five conversations that comprise this book is that they are initiated through the inclusion of papers presented at the C.A.R.N. International Conference 1992 at Worcester College of Higher Education, U.K.. The five 'conversations' in the book begin in the concrete and grounded world of a secondary school classroom in England. Drawing on examples of the way he has confronted aspects of his practice, a teacher is able to set out an argument for a kind of action research with a coherence and logic based upon a dialectical form of educational knowledge. Following this comes an account from the U.S.A., and one focusing on the all too rarely documented world of the action researcher in the operating theatre. The account traces the action researcher's attempts to bring about improvements in the practice of clinical anaesthesia. A powerful and vivid image is conveyed of how the process of action research can lead us into a spiral of ever increasing complexity and depth.

Two accounts from Australia follow. Both relate explicitly to the work of self and others. In the first contribution, a university action researcher takes a critical look at the concept of 'collective autonomy', and argues that this is the golden thread which runs through educational action research. Some of the commitments of Deakin University to action research are set out, and illustrations of these commitments are made by drawing upon the work of teachers and workplace educators associated with action research projects and courses at Deakin. The next account focuses on the experiences of language teachers, and looks at the interplay between the management of self in action research, and the development of a critical understanding of the context in which action research takes place. The researchers make the telling point that even in supportive contexts, action research can be hard to keep going.

Paulo Freire once wrote:

'Without dialogue there is no communication and without communication there can be no true education.' (Freire, P., 1990, ***The Pedagogy of the Oppressed***, p.65). To engage in a meaningful dialogue with others is to understand something of the different ways educational knowledge and experience can be generated, structured and conveyed through different forms of language. This issue is addressed in the last contribution in the book. Here the writer claims that *'it is through story, through narrative of all sorts, that we understand ourselves and our worlds ... My narrative represents who I am, what and who I value and disdain ... My writing sends personal, political and/or ethical messages ... Because of this, what and how I write become crucial to me ... and must be attended to. Awesome!'*

We see the conversations in this book as a moment in an on-going dialogue in our professional worlds about the nature and educative potency of educational action research. We hope that the book stimulates you to engage in conversations of this kind with your own colleagues in your own workplaces. We would be happy to receive accounts of such conversations for distribution through the C.A.R.N. Network. Please send them to the editors in care of:

Tony Ghaye,
School of Education,
Worcester College of Higher Education,
Henwick Grove,
Worcester,
WR2 6AJ
United Kingdom.

INTRODUCING THE EDITORS

TONY GHAYE Reader in Education and Director of Studies: Advanced Professional Modular Scheme, Worcester College of Higher Education

'Life has been a series of surprises for me. At school I was always surprised by my success at the non-academic things when I tried to work so hard at all those curriculum subjects. As a student I was surprised at how much time I had to work hard and play hard if only I could get myself organised, could prioritise and plan properly. When teaching in school, in a variety of other workplaces and in Higher Education, I am constantly surprised and challenged by the extremes of joy and sadness, exhilaration and frustration, that I experience every day.

I was surprised when a headteacher, in passing my study at College, remarked to a friend, "Oh, this is Tony's office. He used to work in school." The other replied, "I didn't realise he had given up teaching!" I have also been surprised at how much pleasure I have been able to derive from one painter, L.S. Lowry, one singer, Witney Houston, one piece of music, namely Turandot by Puccini, one landscape, the rocky seashore at low tide, and one film, **Dances with Wolves.**

I was genuinely surprised to discover that it was only when I was prepared critically to reflect on my practice that I really began to learn about myself and my professional work. I was surprised how far the reversals in my thinking brought about by the work of Robert Chambers, Margot Ely, Paulo Freire, Margaret Mead and Jack Whitehead could be so liberating. I guess these are life's uncelebrated emancipatory moments. I like surprises.'

PETER WAKEFIELD Senior Lecturer: School of Education, Worcester College of Higher Education

'Life has presented me with a number of significant opportunities. In this respect I can count myself as being fortunate that those who guided my progress along unchartered pathways perceived my welfare and success as being of paramount importance. The fact that I have a considerable sense of personal wellbeing and feel proud of my achievements is a testament to those who harnessed my impetuosity and nurtured my desire to improve the quality of life for the more vulnerable members of our society. As a teacher, as a social worker, and headteacher, I attempted to create opportunities for children to acquire success and derive personal satisfaction from their achievements. As a lecturer I have been seduced by the opportunities to reflect upon my practice within a climate of innovation and critical review. Once again I have been introduced to significant others, both within my institution and from the wider world of action enquiry, whose wisdom and creativity have paved the way for those who follow behind with more tentative footsteps. Once again I have been supported and encouraged to feel that as a "beginning" researcher, my experience, my perceptions and my passion for the fulfilment of my visions are credible - I feel positively regarded. The contributions made within this trilogy by those who have shared their experiences, lived out their values before a wider audience, sit comfortably beside those aspiring researchers whose stories have yet to be told. This is their forum, their opportunity - and mine also!'

CONVERSATION ONE

KEVIN EAMES
I started teaching English in 1972, in a secondary modern school which then became comprehensive. Since 1980, I've been head of English at Wootton Bassett School, U.K., apart from secondments of varying lengths (the last one of two years, working for Wiltshire LEA's assessment team).

I've always been interested in reflecting on my own teaching, and developing it (through such channels as Pat D'Arcy's 'Learning about Learning' project in Wiltshire in the early 1980s). In 1984, I registered at Bath University for an MPhil, knowing that classroom-based action research was what I wanted to do. After completing my MPhil, I started getting restless without a bit of regular action research, so I began the work I'm engaged in at the moment, which is looking at how teachers' educational knowledge, developed through collaborative action research, could constitute the professional knowledge which teaching does not yet have.

NICK CLAY
I'm 44 years old and live and work in Cumbria, U.K., where I moved from Suffolk with my family 18 months ago. I've been a secondary school English teacher virtually all my working life, and from the beginning have experienced a fairly constant tension between my social and educational ideals, and the pressures of 'the system'. A growing awareness of the way we adults ignore, manipulate and oppress children has sharpened my interest in the therapeutic potential of educational processes. Increasingly for me 'professional development' and even 'curriculum development' have come to mean 'personal emancipation', and my involvement with action research has been less a matter of acquiring a relevant methodology than of discovering an understanding community. I'm still learning how to relate to that community and desire to extend it, though my effectiveness in doing so would seem inextricably bound up with the way I relate to myself. Hence my commitment to the idea of knowledge as a personal domain and my interest in the role of the feelings in educational enquiry.

A DIALECTICAL FORM OF ACTION RESEARCH-BASED EDUCATIONAL KNOWLEDGE: A TEACHER-RESEARCHER'S VIEW

Kevin Eames

INTRODUCTION

In Hirst's opinion (Hirst, 1983), educational theory is 'concerned with determining rationally defensible principles for educational practice'. In contrast with his earlier view (Hirst, 1966), he argues that 'the adequate formulation and defence of these principles [rests] not simply on appeal to the disciplines, but on a complex pragmatic process that uses its own appropriate practical discourse'. Thus, he places 'the practitioner's view' as central, and applauds the recent 'focus on the actual practices of education, and the discourses practitioners use'.

However, although he senses that the logic of educational theory is bound up with 'the practitioner's view', and the 'actual practices of education', he confesses himself 'uncertain' as to 'how best we might give an account of the logic of such discourse and its principles' (Hirst, 1983). In Part One of this article, I want to show why it seems to me that the 'logic' which Hirst is seeking has a dialectical form. In Part Two, I want to consider why it is significant for the professionality of teachers that the form of logic which constitutes educational knowledge is dialectical. I also want to consider how this view of educational knowledge may be supported and developed in schools.

PART ONE

I want to explain how I see educational knowledge, how I see dialectical knowledge, and how I see the similarities between them, based on a shared logical form. I then want to give examples from my own classroom practice to illustrate what I mean (Eames, 1989a).

1. What Do I See As 'Educational Knowledge'?

Following Peters (1967), I believe that education is a process of growth, of movement; it's a process of amelioration, of change for the better. It's a movement towards enlightenment, towards a more conscious understanding ('The learner must know what he is doing, must be conscious of something he is trying to master, understand or remember': Peters, op.cit.). Educational knowledge, which I see as being constituted by the action-research accounts of reflective practitioners, using a five-part structure (McNiff, 1988/1992), seems to me to share in this movement, for it is knowledge which is educational, in three senses:

(a) the knowledge is constituted from an educational process;
(b) the act of acquiring the knowledge leads towards enlightenment and conscious understanding;
(c) the knowledge itself is knowledge which can educate about education.

Thus, by enquiring into the educational processes occurring in my own classroom, which I am trying to change and improve through the action-research cycles I undertake, and which I am trying to give an account of as a teacher-researcher, I am generating educational knowledge. It is educational because not only is it constituted from an educational process, but also because through methodical enquiry I am moving to a more conscious understanding of my own practice as a teacher. It is also educational because the knowledge thus generated can contribute to further educational processes if it is used by other teachers in their reflections and in their classroom practice.

Just as it is for Hirst, so the concept of practice is central to my definition of educational knowledge, for the educational processes of my classroom practice feed the knowledge I generate, which can then feed the reflections and practice of other teachers, within the framework of a research-based professionality. Such practice-based 'educational knowledge' is distinct from 'knowledge about education', which is not constituted within educational processes in the way I have described above, but is produced by observers of educational processes who are not themselves active participants in what they describe. Knowledge about education can be useful to teachers reflecting and acting on their own practice, and can thus be educational in my third sense ((c) above); but I believe it must be distinguished from educational knowledge itself, because it is not generated by practitioners reflecting on their practice and communicating it within a framework of research-based professionality. Knowledge about education therefore lacks elements (a) and (b) above.

My view here is strongly influenced by Elliott's distinction between 'educational theories' and 'theories about education' (Elliott, 1989). In his account, also, Elliott stresses the complex, organic nature of the educational theories which are formed from practice; they are 'a holistic appreciation of educational practice' which 'cannot be broken down ... without loss of meaning.' Hirst, I think, is also showing awareness of this point when he mentions the complexity of that 'pragmatic process' from which the principles of educational theory can be, in some way, shaped. The logic of educational knowledge needs, then, to be true to this sense of wholeness, of complexity, to catch the interpenetration of theory and practice which happens when my theories about education are continually being used within my classroom practice, and are being modified and transmuted by that practice.

2. What Do I Understand By 'Dialectical Knowledge'?

There are three strands I would like to distinguish in my thinking about dialectical knowledge. The first strand starts with the concept of the dialogue. Schön's phrase about professional knowledge being constituted by 'a reflective conversation with a unique and changing situation' (Schön, 1983) is an important starting point for me, with its assumption that a living, developing dialogue is embodied in the very nature of the way reflective practitioners act and think. Collingwood, referring to Plato, puts forward the view that 'true knowledge' is dialectical, based on 'the interplay of question and answer' (Collingwood, 1924). This view suggests that dialogue is fundamental to a living, developing form of knowledge; Collingwood's comments, too, about the dialectic of art (in which the mind, in its struggle to understand, passes through ' .. the stage in which [its] reach exceeds its grasp, and barely touches a conception as yet undetermined') (Collingwood, op.cit.) seem close to Peters's idea of 'initiation', of helping a learner move from what he/she cannot yet do, to a state where he/she can do it (Peters, 1967).

There seems to me to be an affinity between the educational processes going on in the classrooms of reflective teachers using an action research approach, and the notion of a dialogue. When I as a teacher 'struggle to understand' my own practice, I am engaging in a 'reflective conversation' with what is happening; I am posing questions about the educational processes going on in my classroom, and I am trying to move towards a state of enlightenment, of greater understanding, as a result of my questioning. This process is close to my definition of educational knowledge in the sense of 1(b) above. Likewise the educational processes mentioned in 1(a) above often include questions and answers in the form of dialogues with my pupils, as I seek to tap into their thinking, or seek to prompt them to a higher level of understanding in what they do.

The second strand I wish to distinguish is the idea of the dialogue being a logical form with an ancient lineage. In the examples of dialogue described in the previous paragraph, there is a sense of uncertainty existing within stability. The stability comes from the form, the 'logic of question and answer' which Gadamer says that Collingwood started to develop (Gadamer, 1975). The uncertainty comes from the way in which a question prefigures the leap into the not-yet-known which is an answer. That answer carries understanding a stage further forward (an educational process), and is succeeded by a further question. The answer to each question is unknown, or only dimly apprehended, at the time the question is asked, but each answer goes beyond the question.

When I question my own practice, then, or when I engage in a dialogue with a pupil, I am using a logical form. I don't know for sure what the answer will be, or where it will lead me, but I do know that the logical form will sustain the forward movement of my living, changing understanding. The questions I ask arise from my feeling that what I am doing in the classroom is in some way falling short of what I see as an ideal; I need to improve my own teaching in some way, or I need to prompt my pupils to move onwards from their present state of understanding.

Ilyenkov (1977) describes this state as 'contradiction', which is, he states, 'the real nucleus of dialectics, its central category.' He refers to the concept of the 'living contradiction' which holds within itself, in a unity, both what it is now, and the seeds of what it is to become. By the logic of question and answer, I, a 'living contradiction', existing in the tension between what my practice is now and what I want it to become, can advance to a higher level of understanding or to a more effective state of classroom practice. Comey (1972) describes the process by which I attempt to solve the contradictions I perceive as one of 'negation'. I perceive that my practice does not reach the way I want things to be; it falls short, and is being 'negated'; I therefore take action to solve the contradiction - to 'negate the negation'; this new phase will then give rise to fresh contradictions or negations, which I will take steps to solve or negate, and so on. It's a form that is continually living, changing, developing.

The third strand in my definition is that of practice, which is an essential element in dialectics, as it is in my view of educational knowledge. The questions and answers of the dialectical form already described are not separate from practice; they are part of it, emerging from it, and feeding back into it. When I ask questions about what I'm doing, my answers need to be tested out in action, to see whether they work or not. Ilyenkov makes the point that practice ' ... [is] brought into the logical process as a phase, [is] looked upon as though in its external revelation, in the course of checking its results through direct contact with "things in themselves"' (Ilyenkov, op.cit.).

The relation of question, answer and practice is an organic, unified one, and this difference-within-unity is characteristic of the dialectical form - as it is characteristic of educational knowledge in my account above. When, in Plato's **Phaedrus**, Socrates is discussing the nature of dialectics, he observes that he is 'a great lover of these methods of division and collection ... ' that confer 'the ability to discuss unity and plurality as they exist in the nature of things' (Plato, 1973). Over two thousand years later, Engels, in formulating his 'laws' of dialectics, speaks of this logical form as 'the science of inter-connections' (Engels, 1934). Comey, too, sees the way in which the dialectical form necessarily contains 'opposing elements' which, however, 'form an interrelated polarity so that they presuppose and reciprocally affect each other'. The tensions between these elements (the contradictions, for example, that I perceive in my practice) 'provide the impetus for change and development; resolution of the conflict is accompanied by progression to a new stage of development of the thing.' (Comey, op.cit.).

3. The Dialectical Form of Educational Knowledge

Putting these two sections together, it seems to me that the similarities between my view of educational knowledge, and my view of dialectics, are strong. Educational knowledge (that is, the knowledge of practice which I as a classroom practitioner have generated through an action research cycle) has dialectical elements within it because:

(a) In both cases, there is a movement towards enlightenment, towards understanding. In this movement towards understanding, dialogue is of central importance.
(b) In both cases, there is a question and answer structure. The logical form of question and answer gives a sustaining sense of uncertainty-within-stability within which I can address myself to the contradictions I identify within my practice.
(c) In both cases, there is a close and complex relation with practice. The educational processes of my classroom practice feed the knowledge I generate through an action research cycle, and that knowledge in turn informs the next action research cycle which develops as a result of what I have learnt in the previous cycle. Similarly, the questions and answers of the dialectical form are

not separate from practice; they are part of it, emerging from it and feeding back into it. This sense of wholeness, of complexity in the educational knowledge which is derived from practice, gives a characteristically organic sense of difference-within-unity which is captured by the dialectical form's concept of contradiction.

Educational knowledge and dialectics are not identical, for dialectics is a form of logic with a tradition of its own which existed long before the kind of educational knowledge I'm talking about here came into being. They both, however, seem to me to share characteristics as I've described above. When Hirst says that he is seeking an underpinning logic for what he calls 'educational theory', I wonder whether that logic is dialectical in form, for dialectics in practice is an embodiment of logic; it unites the concept of a theoretical logic with the discourses and actions of practitioners, to constitute a form of educational knowledge where theory and practice are inseparable. Perhaps Hirst was closer than he realised to uncovering the logic he was searching for, when he suggested that we look to the 'actual practice of education, and the discourses practitioners use'?

4. *What Evidence Do I Have For This View Of Educational Knowledge?*

A problem with the educational knowledge generated by action research is its complex, organic nature. It's difficult to present it in summarised form without wrenching it from its context, without interrupting the narrative flow, and thus, as Elliott says (Elliott, op.cit.), losing meaning. However, I think it's necessary to run that risk in order to illustrate the argument I've been advancing. More detailed accounts of the evidence I give can be found elsewhere (Eames, 1989b/1991).

I have tried to demonstrate the dialectical form of educational knowledge by, first, looking at two action research cycles from my own classroom to see if a dialectical form is perceptible in the account which I gave. Second, I have looked at how my account of these two cycles was used by a group of five teachers and other educators in the area where I work to see, again, if a dialectical form is perceptible, not just in my own practice, but with a wider group, in the way my action research accounts were used and discussed. In this section, I will examine my account of the action research cycles from my own classroom.

The first action research cycle from my own classroom gave an account of an attempt I made to improve the quality of pupils' reflections on, and understanding of, their own writing. I concentrated, in particular, on Stephen, a lower-attaining male student, for it was this category which seemed to benefit less than other pupils from the English faculty's policy of asking pupils to reflect upon and review their learning at the end of each unit of GCSE coursework.

Having identified an area which I wanted to improve, I formulated possible solutions to the problem I saw, which involved departing from our normal practice. Instead of giving pupils a prompt-sheet containing questions they might ask about their writing, and letting them work through the sheet at their own pace, I decided to select appropriate questions from the prompt-sheet myself, and ask pupils to answer them, under pressure of time, in bursts of silent 'think-writing'.

The increase in length and quality of Stephen's written review revealed a depth of understanding about his writing that I had been unaware of until then. However, it also revealed that Stephen was much more specific in his comments on transcription than on the compositional aspects of his writing. In addition, he seemed unable to acknowledge the growth in his learning between coursework units. This was, I thought, partly because I hadn't explained clearly enough to him the difference between these two aspects of writing, and partly because, as my reflections on the action research cycle brought home to me, I was asking him to perform a highly abstract task which he was finding difficult.

Accordingly, I replanned my actions. I asked Stephen to set himself a composition target for improvement in his next piece of writing, basing the target on some aspect of his coursework in the past that he wanted to improve. He said that he wanted to use more detail in his writing, in order, as he said, to 'give a complete impression to the reader'. Also, influenced by the work of Ann Berthoff (Berthoff, 1981), and by my reflections at the end of the previous action research cycle, I asked him to write a commentary on his draft as it was developing, explaining how he was trying to put into practice his intention of giving a 'complete impression to the reader'. I wanted him to do this so that it would keep his attention focused on the target he had set, and would bring, so I hoped, his thinking to a level of more conscious control.

As events turned out, Stephen's draft suggested that he seemed to have kept his target in mind, for the improvement in his use of detail was marked. However, he seemed unable to express objectively what he had done in order to achieve his target, for he was most reluctant to write a commentary on his draft, and, when he finally did (to keep me quiet, I suspect), it held no references to the target I had asked him to consider, and consisted mainly of expressions of satisfaction with what he had achieved.

Although I, too, was happy with Stephen's achievement, I felt that the draft could be improved more than he had acknowledged. Later, when I talked to him, he showed that he could identify many more areas for improvement than he had done, earlier, in the commentary he had written - although in some cases, he needed prompting to be specific about what needed doing, and how. Finally, Stephen was left with an improved piece of writing, and I was left with more questions to carry back into my classroom practice. Why was he able to identify areas for improvement in dialogue with me, but didn't, or couldn't do it by himself, in his commentary? Was it because the writing had been lying fallow for some days and he'd had a chance to think about it? Was it because he thinks better in dialogue than in writing, or simply that he knew I wouldn't let him off the hook until he'd delivered a plan for improving his draft? Why didn't he want to write about his developing draft? Did he not understand what I wanted him to do? Had I not explained it clearly enough, or did he see it as interfering with his enjoyment of the developing draft? Was it too complex a task for the stage he had reached? How far, in fact, do I understand the relationship between what a pupil can do, and his conscious awareness of what he is doing (for the educational knowledge I'd been guided by previously didn't seem to work in this 'unique case" - to use Schön's phrase (Schön, 1983).

In trying to explain why I think the action research accounts summarised above embody a dialectical form of thinking and acting, I will take as a guide the three areas of similarity between educational knowledge and dialectics which I pointed out in 3(a), (b) and (c) above.

(a) In the two action research cycles I have described, there seems to be a movement, through dialogue, towards enlightenment and understanding. I have moved towards enlightenment and understanding since I now know that cutting down on the number of questions to be answered, and writing under pressurised conditions, have brought to the surface, on Stephen's part, a previously undisplayed understanding of writing. I know, too, that setting a specific target for improvement worked, but I couldn't get to the bottom of why it worked - and the strategy I was relying on to make it work had, apparently, no effect at all on the outcome. Also, the educational knowledge I was drawing on when I asked Stephen to write a commentary on his developing draft didn't seem to apply in this case, for Stephen avoided doing as I had asked, but nevertheless seemed to have improved his writing in line with the target he had set himself. Whatever enlightenment I have achieved is local, embodied in this unique case.

It's also knowledge which is provisional and continually shifting; in the account given above, I identified an area I wanted to change, worked out possible solutions which would improve my practice, took action, and evaluated what happened. Some aspects of what I was trying to do were successful; in each of the action research cycles, however, new problems were revealed, and new questions posed when I reflected on what had happened - and so into a new cycle. This provisional quality comes, I think, from the very form of knowing and acting which is action research. It forces me, as an action researcher, into a dialogue with my practice, asking questions to which I propose answers, which initiate action, which leads to a provisional understanding, which is partially formed of more questions. It's the dialogue with my own practice which drives the process within which I move to a state of knowing more about my teaching, in no matter how provisional a way.

(b) Because this forward movement through dialogue is a process of question and answer, it is in itself a logical form, characteristic of dialectical logic. The process of question and answer is inherent in the structure of the action research cycle, a form of knowing and acting which thus embodies the logic of dialectics. By reflecting on my practice through action research, therefore, I am thinking and acting dialectically, as I question my practice and identify an area I am not satisfied with (lower-attaining male students, such as Stephen, don't handle the process of reviewing their learning as effectively as most other students); I propose answers to the problems I have identified (I select the questions myself, and ask pupils to complete reviews silently under 'think-writing' conditions); I take action; I question the results of that action (Stephen's review is much longer and reveals an unexpected depth of understanding, although he finds it easier to focus on transcription rather than on composition; also, he seems unable to acknowledge development from one coursework piece to the next); I propose answers to the problems that have now been revealed (I ask him to set a composition target based on what he wanted to improve in his previous work; I ask him to write a commentary on his draft as it develops, so he can keep his target in mind).

Ilyenkov's 'central category of dialectics' - contradiction - is detectable here, too. I exist as a 'living contradiction' (Ilyenkov, 1977), in that I am inhabiting a classroom practice which I find unsatisfactory in the way I have described, while, at the same time, I can imagine an improved level of practice which has overcome the problems I am aware of. From the tension between the two opposing poles of this contradiction (where I am now, and where I want to be) come the proposed solutions, which are then embodied in action, as previously explained.

(c) The role of practice in this view of educational knowledge is illustrated by the way in which my original dissatisfaction is revealed by my reflections on what was happening in my classroom - the difficulties certain pupils were experiencing with reviewing their work. My own classroom practice thus forms the original focus for the action research process. I propose solutions, based on what I already understand about children's learning (selected questions: 'think-writing') and I feed those understandings back into my practice in the actions I take. The understandings which emerge from my actions are themselves used to inform the next cycle of reflection and action (Stephen's review has improved in length, and in the quality of the understanding demonstrated. However, I have become aware that he finds difficulty in expressing his understanding of composition, and in acknowledging development from piece to piece, and so I formulate proposed solutions to these newly-emerged problems).

The complexity, the organic 'difference-within-unity' which I have said is characteristic of the dialectical form (3(c) above), is captured by the notion of contradiction. Within the unity of what I am, I am teaching in a way which brings about an undesirable effect (lower-attaining pupils in my classroom, such as Stephen, find difficulties in reviewing their own writing) while at the same time I want to do something to improve it. These two 'polarities' (Comey, 1972) of the contradiction which I am living are an organic unity because one would not exist without the other; my desire to improve my practice wouldn't exist if I were unaware of the undesirable effect of what I was already doing. By using the action research cycle, I can express something of a classroom's real complexity - the tension between the two polarities of the contradiction which I am living; the proposed solutions which emerge as an attempt to solve the contradictions (select questions; use of 'think-writing'); the new contradictions which then emerge (although Stephen's reviewing has improved, I have become aware that he finds difficulty in expressing his understanding of composition, and in acknowledging development from piece to piece), and which lead into the next cycle.

PART TWO

I now want to consider why it is significant for the professionality of teachers that the form of logic which constitutes educational knowledge is dialectical. I also want to consider how this form of educational knowledge may be supported and developed in schools.

1. Why Is This View Of Educational Knowledge Significant For Teachers' Professionality?

(a) If, as I have tried to demonstrate, the underlying logic of educational knowledge, as constituted by teachers' action research accounts of their classroom practice, is a dialectical logic, then we have what Hirst was asking for in the account of his argument which I gave in the introduction to this paper. We have a form of 'practical discourse', constituted by the 'practitioner's view' and the 'discourses which practitioners use' (Hirst, 1983), which now can be acknowledged to have a coherent form of logic at the centre of it. And if that is so, we have a form of educational knowledge which can embody the professional knowledge which teaching, at the moment, lacks (Beyer, 1987; Brownhill, 1983).

Hitherto, the educational knowledge of teachers has been seen as being of lower status than the propositional form of knowledge about education which has been located mainly in universities. While I am not denying the usefulness of such propositional knowledge about education, I believe that a useful way of regarding its relation to teachers' educational knowledge, up to now, is to see the latter as analogous to Foucault's category of 'subjugated knowledges' - 'local' and 'low-ranking', existing 'parallel' to the higher-status form of propositional knowledge about education, but 'marginal' to it (Foucault, 1980). If teachers' educational knowledge can be accepted as having a logical form which is equal in status to the propositional form (and I believe that dialectics, with its ancient lineage, is such a form) then the first leg of a research-based professional knowledge produced by teachers and for teachers is in place.

However, apart from the coherent rationale which the dialectical form provides, there are two other legs needed before the edifice is securely founded:

(b) To provide the second leg, the accounts produced must communicate to and be usable by other teachers. To illustrate this point, I will take one example from the interviews I carried out with five teachers and other educators, who had read the action research account of my work with Stephen (Part One, Section 4 above), and with whom I discussed the ways in which their practice had been influenced (or not) by the paper. Andy Larter, who is head of English at Greendown School, Swindon, and a fellow action researcher, was positive that, in his view, the paper had been of use to him, and had influenced his classroom practice:

> *'I've ripped off some of your ideas, Kev. This review sheet I've taken on as being a really good idea. And I've used it with a couple of kids in my fourth year.'*

Interestingly, Andy made use of the ideas in a manner that transmuted my original account of my practice, adapting the basic 'reviewing' format to his own, local needs in developing a structure for pupils' 'enquiry groups' in his integrated humanities class:

> *'I've tried this as an experiment, to prove a point, though, in school, and what I've done is to set up ... enquiry groups ... for integrated humanities ... '*

He had also found the paper useful as a focus for discussion (*'I've already talked about it with Erica, and the people I work with in the team'*), and expressed an intention to give it wider circulation:

> *'I'm going to photocopy it and pass it round. I'll pass it to Erica, who's another team leader, and the members of my team, and she'll distribute it to her team as well, so there'll be plenty of people reading it and thinking about reviewing and what it means.'*

In the view of this teacher, then, an action research account, in the dialectical form which I have previously described, has been of use in his own classroom, and in providing an agenda for discussion with colleagues.

(c) Finally, the dialectical form must be a shared form - not just detectable in my own practice, but something which appears, characteristically, in 'the discourse practitioners use' (Hirst, 1983). I have already (Part One, Section 4(c)) tried to explain the way in which the dialectical form of an action research account can capture, within its narratives and its concept of contradiction, the organic complexities of a teacher's living, changing educational knowledge. From the interviews I recorded (Part Two, Section 1(b)), I should like to give one example, as illustration of another teacher existing as a living contradiction, and reflecting dialectically upon her practice.

Daniela De Cet is an English faculty colleague at Wootton Bassett School, and a fellow action researcher. After she had read the account of my work with Stephen, she discussed the paper with me, and, at one point in the transcript, related it to a problem she had identified in her own practice. She, too, was aware of the problem which had emerged in the action research cycles with Stephen, but pointed out a further complexity, that asking pupils to review the targets set in their previous piece of coursework might be inappropriate, since they might have been working on a different kind of writing:

> *'... With the kind of coursework we do, I find it quite difficult to look back at the content, the targets they've set themselves and so on ... It's quite difficult in that they're trying to do something completely different.'*

Here are similar features to those identified in my own practice (part One, Section 4 above). Daniela has questioned her own practice, and realises that she exists in a state of contradiction. Accordingly, she sets out to give an answer which resolves that contradiction:

> *'What about something, then ... couldn't you ... instead of trying always to have a step-by-step development, have a point, looking back ... trying to trace their development after a certain point, rather than trace it as it's going along? ... That could be after maybe three or four pieces of coursework ... or maybe at the end of term - to look back and set the targets maybe for next term, when ... they're likely to be ... asked to use things that they've covered, again ... I'd quite like to try that out, actually, to see if it works.'*

The whole process of question, answer, contradiction and resolution is conceived in terms of her own practice - starting from it ('I find it quite difficult ...') and ending, in this extract, with an expressed intention to try out her proposed solution, 'to see if it works'. In the way in which she reflects on her practice, then, Daniela shares the dialectical form of thinking and planning action.

2. How Can This Form Of Educational Knowledge Be Supported And Developed In Schools?

If the argument I am advancing makes sense, and teachers' action research accounts of their own practice are appropriate as a professional form of research-based educational knowledge, how can we take action to ensure that this form is generally accepted and used? I have already written elsewhere (Eames, 1990) about my own development as an action researcher, and the developments at Wootton Bassett School; but in this section, I should like to make some general reflections on practical ways of supporting action research as a professional form of educational knowledge.

(a) Individual action researchers are the seed from which the harvest of research-based professionality will come. In my own case, the ground had been thoroughly prepared by the Wiltshire English adviser, Pat D'Arcy, and her 'Learning About Learning' project, which enabled teachers to share their practice with critically supportive colleagues, to investigate what was going on in their own classrooms, and to make public their accounts of practice (Wiltshire LEA). Pat D'Arcy, as an extension of 'Learning About Learning' encouraged me and another member of the project (Andy Larter) to register at Bath University for MPhil Degrees, and organised the support of the LEA in the form of supply cover and help with fees. The agreement of the head teachers at our respective schools was essential, and the existence of another researcher with whom to discuss work in progress was of great value.

(b) The support I received from Jack Whitehead at Bath University was essential in making me realise that action research was not just yet another name for classroom research, but a form of investigation and communication with its own coherence and logic, which seemed to me appropriate to the way I worked in and reflected on my classroom. Jack Whitehead, and the university, provided the 'quality control' in ensuring that our accounts (Eames, 1987; Larter, 1987) met the accepted standards by which academic work is judged, and I feel that it is important to stress the indispensible role of the university in giving rigour and credibility to the work of action researchers. The further qualifications awarded by the university are essential to any scheme of research-based professionality which has in mind the continuing, career-long development of teachers.

(c) Once individual action researchers are confident in their own understanding of what they are doing, they can support groups of other action researchers in their own sphere of influence. Here are three variations on this theme:

—**An inter-school, cross-phase group:** Pat D'Arcy, the Wiltshire English adviser, has, over the past two and a half years, co-ordinated successive groups of primary and secondary teachers who have been working towards Certificates and Diplomas in Professional Development at Bath University, where they have held regular meetings to discuss progress. Funding has come from two sources - the LEA's advisers' budget, and schools' devolved INSET budgets.

—**A group of researchers within a single school:** At Wootton Bassett School, Swindon, a group of researchers (one from each faculty) is registered for Diplomas in Professional Development at Bath University (*Times Educational Supplement*, 6 September, 1990; ***Research Intelligence,*** No. 37, pp.24-26: British Educational Research Association). The teachers are working on putting into practice some aspect of their faculties' contributions to the school's development plan, and on evaluating it. Support from senior management and heads of faculties for an action research approach to the school's development was established at a one day conference in January, 1990. Before the conference, the Bassett Action Research Group had existed as a group of researchers within the school who supported each other through informal meetings and contacts, and published occasional papers or collections of papers (Eames, 1989c). Funding, again, is a mixture, with the LEA paying for registration at Bath, and the school providing from its own budget half a day's remitted time per week for each teacher. At Greendown School, Swindon, the researchers are registered at Bath for MPhil and PhD Degrees, and the school is funding registration fees from its devolved INSET budget. The head teachers at both schools are strongly supportive. At Greendown, the head teacher is a member of the research group (*Times Educational Supplement*, 22 March, 1991; *Research Intelligence*, No. 37, pp.24-26: BERA).

—A group of PGCE students researching their teaching practice: Moira Laidlaw, at Bath University, is working with students who wish to give action research accounts of their educational development on teaching practice (Laidlaw, 1991).

CONCLUSION

If the five part action research cycle, with its dialectical form, is the practitioner-based form of educational knowledge towards which Hirst's thoughts were turning, and if it can stand as a professional form of knowledge by teachers and for teachers, we've made a start in moving teaching towards becoming a profession in its own right. It's necessary to do that, I think, because teachers, and teacher educators, are under serious political attack (Lawlor, 1990). We need a research base, by teachers and for teachers, but with the rigour and credibility which comes from higher education involvement, if we are to resist the attacks of the ignorant and the politically doctrinaire by demonstrating the successes of reflective teachers in improving their practice. The accounts produced by action researchers need circulating among teachers, and should contribute in some way to a growing archive of classroom-based educational knowledge. Local circulation is already happening (for example, Part Two, Section 1(b) above) but some form of communication which enables teachers to read about action research by other teachers is lacking, I feel. How can we fill that gap? How can the existing databases of research summaries be made more available to teachers? How can we carry forward the argument that all teachers should reflect on ways of improving their classroom practice, as a necessary part of their professional responsibilities - and should have the time and the support to do it? How, in fact, do we make research-based professionality, as the cornerstone of a general teaching council, a reality, rather than a question in an academic journal?

References

Berthoff, A., *The Making of Meaning* (Boynton Cook, New Jersey, 1981).

Beyer, L., 'What knowledge is of most worth in teacher education?' in Smyth, J., *Educating Teachers: Changing the Nature of Pedagogical Knowledge* (Falmer Press, Sussex, 1987).

Brownhill, R.J., *Education and the Nature of Knowledge* (Croom Helm, Chapter 10, 1983).

Collingwood, R.G., *Speculum Mentis, or The Map of Knowledge* (Clarendon Press, Oxford, 1924).

Comey, D.D., 'Logic' in Kernig, *Marxism, Communism and Western Society* (Harder and Harder, New York, 1972).

Eames, K., *The Growth of a Teacher-Researcher's Attempt to Understand Writing, Redrafting, Learning and Autonomy in the Examination Years* (MPhil Dissertation, University of Bath, 1987).

Eames, K., 'Dialogues and Dialectics': a paper presented at the International Conference of the Collaborative Action Research Network, University of East Anglia, 1989(a); later published in Edwards, G. and Rideout, P. (Eds), *Extending the Horizons of Action Research* (CARN Publication 10C, 1991).

Eames, K., '*Personal Growth Through Students Reviewing Their Own Writing*' (Bassett Action Research Group, Wootton Bassett School, Swindon, Wiltshire, 1989(b)).

Eames, K. (ed.), '*How can we Improve Professionalism in Education Through Collaborative Action Research?*' (Bassett Action Research Group, Wootton Bassett School, Swindon, Wiltshire, 1989c).

Eames, K. 'Growing Your Own' in British Journal of In-Service Education, Vol. 16, No. 2, pp.122-127, Autumn, 1990; Reprinted in McNiff, J., *Teaching as Learning: an Action Research Approach* (Routledge, London and New York, 1993).

Elliott, J., 'Educational theory and the professional learning of teachers: an overview' in Cambridge Journal of Education, Vol. 19, No. 1, (1989).

Engels, F., *Dialectics of Nature* (Progress Publishers, Moscow, 1934).

Foucault, M., *Power/Knowledge* (Harvester Press, Sussex, 1980).

Gadamer, H.G., *Truth and Method* (New York, Seabury Press, 1975).

Hirst, P.H., 'Educational Theory' in Tibble, J.W. (ed.), *The Study of Education* (London, Routledge and Kegan Paul, 1966).

Hirst, P.H., 'Educational Theory' in Hirst, P.H., *Educational Theory and Its Foundation Disciplines'* (London, Routledge and Kegan Paul, 1983).

Ilyenkov, E.V., *Dialectical Logic* (Moscow, Progress Publishers, 1977).

Laidlaw, M., *Action Research: A Guide for Use on Second Teaching Practice* (mimeographed handbook, University of Bath, 1991).

Larter, A.P., *An Action-Research Approach to Classroom Discussion in the Examination Years.* (MPhil Dissertation, University of Bath, 1987).

Lawlor, S., *Teachers Mistaught - Training in Theories of Education in Subjects* (Centre for Policy Studies, 1990).

McNiff, J., *Action Research: Principles and Practice* (Macmillan Education, 1988; Routledge, London and New York, 1992).

Peters, R.S., 'What is an educational process?' in Peters, R.S. (ed.), *The Concept of Education* (London, Routledge and Kegan Paul, 1967).

Plato *Phaedrus* (trans. Hamilton, W., London, Penguin, 1973).

Research Intelligence: Newsletter of the British Educational Research Association (No. 37, 1990).

Schön, D., *The Reflective Practitioner* (Basic Books, New York, 1983).

Times Educational Supplement (6th September, 1990); Times Educational Supplement (22nd March, 1991).

WHAT I WOULD LIKE TO DISCUSS WITH YOU

Nick Clay

Dear Kevin,

I'm writing this 'review' as a letter, because it seems to fit with the innovative dialogic structure of this publication; it seems entirely congruent with the advocacy of dialectic which is the central thrust of your paper; and because it embodies my own view of the personal nature of knowledge.

I found your paper hard to get into, but very engaging once I did. To me your logic seems tightly argued and very clearly structured, though I'm left with a slight sense that the whole thesis is almost too neatly held together by its own internal consistency. I haven't read Hirst, or many of the other theorists you refer to (which no doubt accounts for some of my problem with access) but I'm thoroughly convinced by your central assertions that educational theory and knowledge as constituted by action researchers is dialectical in nature and that this does provide an appropriate and respectable logical basis for the professional development of teachers and enhancement of their status. And I wholeheartedly agree with the recommendations at the conclusion of your paper that we urgently need a more accessible archive for action research accounts to be circulating amongst teachers. (CARN is currently working on this idea, as I'm sure you're aware.) I also fully endorse your desire for a research-based professionality to be the norm and a reality 'rather than a question in an academic journal'.

You present that desire, though, as a question - 'How, in fact, do we ...' - and though I can accept the importance of the theoretical groundwork which makes up the bulkier first part of your paper, and concur that it does provide a vital 'leg' for our professional integrity, it seems to me that it is in the promoting of the other two 'legs', communicative/usable accounts and shared discourse, that a possible answer can be found. You don't give a lot of space to those, and what you do say in Part Two, Section 2, while encouraging in itself, and reminding me that there is a lot happening in different parts of the country, nonetheless leaves me wondering, 'For how long?' (given the economic and political pressures on schools and universities) and whether it's very much 'the lucky few' who benefit ('...the school providing from its own budget half a day's remitted time per week for each teacher.') Wow! I wish I could offer a fraction of that to my overloaded department whom I'm encouraging to develop 'critical friend' partnerships.) Are you managing to continue the ongoing discourse and set up fresh action research cycles this year, in the face of statutory appraisal, changes to the GCSE syllabuses and KS3 SATS? (I'm assuming from the content of your paper that, like me, you're an English teacher.) What do you regard as the most influential in-school factors in sustaining and disseminating action research discourse? My conjecture is that it has a lot to do with you - who you are as a person and how you come across to others, your energy level and work habits, and so on - but that reflects my own interest in the role of the self in action research (and in learning in general) and my excitement with the current focus by some action researchers on the role of feelings in the action research process.

I'm interested in the feeling of the text in your paper. I'm aware that a current preoccupation with some action researchers has been to find alternative forms for reporting their work. Did you give any thought to this in preparing your paper? You acknowledge at the beginning of Part One, Section 4, that there's a risk of losing something: organic complexity? narrative flow? meaning? - how do these relate to each other and how important are they? I did feel a certain remoteness in your text, even when describing your work with Stephen, which introduced a school context highly familiar to me but somehow denied a texture into which I could completely enter. Even in the burst of new questions raised with which you round off your summary, I'm left with a sense of the ease with which the process of writing itself and the heritage of traditional discourse impose an order, a detachment and a stasis which put the experience being mediated at a stage removed from my own immediate concerns. This changes, though, with the quotes from Andy Larter, which, brief as they are, introduced the authentic immediacy and orientation of real school life. The felt life was there. The question that occurs to me is: should all our discourse have that quality? Would it be appropriate for the kind of intellectual theorising with which your paper opens? I want to ask you what you perceived as the most dominant purpose behind the writing of your paper, and whom did you imagine yourself addressing? Is there another dialectical contradiction lurking here, that we desire recognition and authentication of our own espoused mode of being, yet we are forced by pragmatism to seek it from and through forms that tend to perpetuate an alienating existence? I note what seems to me to be a tension within your paper whereby on the one hand you want to liberate educational discourse from the propositional-removed-from-practice domination associated with the universities, while on the other hand you acknowledge the 'indispensible role of the university in giving rigour and credibility to the work of action researchers.'

Much of what I've written so far has emerged in the process of writing, but my reference to 'propositional-removed-from-practice' discourse reminds me of the issue with which I found myself the most engaged while I was in actual process of reading your paper. It's this distinction you make, quoting John Elliott, between 'educational knowledge' and 'knowledge about education'. It's a distinction which I recognise and have found helpful in thinking about teaching and learning. It perhaps accounts for the widespread disregard of educational research by practising teachers, and I relate it also to my perception that while there have been enormous changes in recent years within actual classroom practice towards experiential and interactive modes of learning, these are widely seen by educators as changes of method and pedagogy, so that the fundamental shift required in our epistemology has barely begun. It's a distinction I think I first encountered in relation to literature: Lawrence in a marvellous passage talking about all the 'pseudo-critical twiddle-twaddle' of knowledge about literature being so much impertinence if it is divorced from an honest, fully felt response to the text. Yet as soon as I draw this parallel with literature I'm aware of a problem, since in this context I don't find the relation to practice so critical. Although it certainly helps, I don't believe it is essential for a student of literature to be a practising creative writer in order to 'connect' in a living way with the meanings which literature embodies. So to return to educational knowledge, is it the practice-centredness that gives authentication (as your thesis centrally proposes), or is it some other factor? Are theory and practice as inseparable as you claim? What happens as accounts of action research get disseminated? **In practice,** isn't it difficult to establish any clear demarcation between 'practitioners reflecting on their practice and communicating it within a framework of research-based professionality' and 'observers of educational processes who are not themselves active participants?' In what sense 'active', or 'participant'? It seems to me that many of us move in and out of these categories. Is our educational knowledge, then, something that intensifies and fades as we move in and out of different modes of activity and relationship, rather like the influence of a magnetic field? To me it actually does feel like that at times. But that means it is far too elusive an entity to be defined by my practice, unless my practice itself is so inclusively defined as to be of little use.

There's more I'd like to tease out here, but space doesn't permit. I'm left with a sense that there's less a philosophical imperative that educational knowledge be rooted in practice, than a political one, given, as you rightly say, the current serious political attack on teachers. I want to argue that the crucial distinguishing feature of what you define as educational knowledge has less to do with its grounding in practice or its difference from knowledge about education than it has with some quality of initiation such as is alluded to at the beginning of ***Creating a Good Social Order Through Action Research*** (McNiff et al, 1992), and I'm fascinated by the parallels she draws with religious experience. But that's the substance of another dialogue. Over to you.

Thanks for writing your paper (into the unknown, not knowing it would lead to this, but sustained by the logic of dialectics!). It's been fruitful for me to make this response; I hope it will provide something in return.

With best wishes,

Yours,

Nick Clay.

References

McNiff, J., Whitehead, J., and Laidlaw, M., and Members of the Bath Action Research Group, *Creating A Good Social Order Through Action Research* (Hyde Publications, Dorset, 1992).

AND IN REPLY

Kevin Eames

Dear Nick,

Thanks for the letter. Yes, it does fit with the dialogical structure of the publication, and I immediately felt comfortable with it. We've never met, but behind your written communication, I sensed a person with the kind of openness that I now believe to be essential in dialogue, and with the educational and social values that I hold.

Thanks for the encouraging comments about the paper. I regard it now as representing a stage in my thinking, and there are many things I'm not happy with - things that you've put your finger on, straight away. You're right about the form in which I wrote at the time. It is remote, detached, and lacks the 'authentic immediacy and orientation of real school life'. You made me think, too, about the reason why you found my description of the work I did with Stephen difficult to get into. I wonder whether it's because I fragmented the story - selected bits from it - and by doing so broke the 'organic complexity and narrative flow' that I think the original account displays.

You're right, also, about the audience and purpose for the paper having an effect on the 'feeling of the text'. It was written in that sort of way because I was writing to a word limit, with the intention of communicating as tightly and concisely as possible the view of educational knowledge that I had at that time. It was propositional in form because I was writing for academic researchers at the conference, and because I had no idea then that it would become part of a dialogical exchange (although I'm delighted that it has). Another reason was that I hadn't started thinking about how to present accounts of my educational development. At the time, I saw the idea of educational knowledge as relating purely to the logical form, and my research carried me for some time along this path, searching for a dialectical shape in the ways that my work with Stephen had been used in the community of teacher researchers in this area. Unfortunately, the more I wandered along this purely academic path, the further I went from real dialogue, and the more isolated my research grew from my own practice as an educator. What I had missed completely was the engagement with a community that is necessary for real dialogue to take place; we need people to talk to - or write to - if our ideas are going to be developed dialectically, for dialectics is social, not solipsistic.

I'd like to think further about your questions concerning the role of practice. When I drew the distinction between 'practitioners reflecting on their practice and communicating it within a framework of research-based professionality' and 'observers of educational processes who are not themselves active participants', I was thinking, on the one hand, of action researchers reflecting on their own practice as researchers or teachers, and giving accounts of how they had developed or improved what they were doing, and what they had learnt in so doing. On the other hand, I was thinking of the traditional kind of research project which does research on teachers, and where the researchers don't reflect on the development of their own practice as researchers. I'm not saying that this second type of research isn't useful; it is, for politicians, managers and so on, and it can also be informative for teachers. However, it is positivist in form, and the researchers tend to hide behind a constructed impersonality. It's also often alienating to teachers, who are put off by the impersonality, by the language employed, and by the implied power structure of such research, which puts teachers into an inferior position. (These points were made to me very forcibly by a group of teachers who criticised the paper we're discussing now, showing me that they felt alienated by the propositional form that I was using.) Educational action research, to me, moves the learning of the researcher to the centre of attention. It's more personal, and, because it's dialectical, it can embody the incompleteness, the messiness of real practice. It's not cut and dried, like traditional propositional research (or like the paper we're discussing at the moment!)

I liked your image of the magnetic field. It captures that shifting, changing, living quality of the educational knowledge I feel inside my own head. To me, it becomes more or less intense as I focus upon particular areas of the complex practice I'm within; sometimes I reflect rigorously, and collect evidence, but often I don't. I just do things or change things without articulating my reasons fully. Practice, I think, is what I do in the classroom or in any other aspect of my work as an educator. According to the way I see the magnetic field that is educational knowledge, it intensifies when I'm thinking about aspects of my practice in a consciously articulated way, and fades when I don't. When it's intense, my thinking about practice is conscious and communicable. It's articulated, so I can talk to others about my thinking, as part of a dialogue. Practice is inseparable from this knowledge, because my knowledge starts from what I do, and I feed my developed understanding back into my practice as a teacher/staff developer/researcher. Does that explain more clearly how I see the relationship between my practice and my educational knowledge? Is it, perhaps, that my view of educational knowledge regards it as something articulated, public, which can be built into a professional knowledge-base, whereas your image of the magnetic field is a more fundamental description of the continually developing personal knowledge we carry around inside our heads? Is it simply that we've emphasised different stages which educational knowledge goes through as it develops? Should we be talking about pluralistic 'knowledges' rather than one monolithic 'knowledge'?

I'd like to pick up another question which I found thought-provoking - the one you raise about the tension between my desire to 'liberate educational discourse from the propositional-removed-from-practice domination associated with the universities, (and my acknowledgement of) the "indispensable role of the university in giving rigour and credibility to the work of action researchers"'. Yes, there is a tension there, and it certainly affected the form I chose for the paper on dialectics, as I've already suggested in my comments about the audience I had in mind when I was writing it. It's not a tension I can easily resolve, but what I'm trying to clarify is the necessity for a professional form of knowledge to have academic acceptance and credibility. It's a question of status and power, for the university needs to legitimate a professional form of knowledge, to give it high status; that's the pattern of professions in our kind of society. However, a dialectical form of knowledge, which can express provisionality within a dialogical community, is a form in which power is distributed equally among the members of the community, who all have a right to be heard in the dialogue, and to learn from it. The power in this dialogue, for instance, is perfectly evenly distributed between us, as we try to tease out our understandings and learn from each other. There's no room for point-scoring or power-wielding in this form, as Peter Mellett (an action researcher at Bath) pointed out to me, in contrast to the propositional form, in which knowledge moves from university theoreticians (high status) to classroom practitioners (low status). This kind of university-located knowledge is, as you know, profoundly alienating for most teachers, whereas I think that a form which involves teachers in dialogue is far more teacher-friendly, but still needs to be understood, accepted and accredited by universities if it is to be considered as a professional form. I hope my explanation doesn't sound too confused to you - as if I'm trying to eat my cake and have it. I'm trying to be practical about the realities of power and status in our society. Does that make sense?

Which brings me to the final issue I've got time and space to respond to. How do we make a dialectical form of knowledge work in a professional sense? Here are a few ideas for your consideration:

◆ We need to carry on the debate about what a professional form of educational knowledge looks like, because, at present, there is no generally-accepted understanding of what it is. I'll send you some work I've recently done on trying to define more clearly a dialectical, action research-based form of knowledge which could be used as a professional form. I'd be interested in your comments.

◆ We need to carry on using action research in our own schools, as we're both trying to do. We can get it accepted into the consciousness of our colleagues that collaborative action research, within a community that talks about it and uses it, is a powerful means of evaluating the school development plan, and an essential element in the appraisal of teachers. Building evaluation by action research into the development plan is probably the most practical way of providing remitted time for researchers, who may then submit their work for accreditation if they wish to do so. However, you need a good headteacher who supports action research, and we're lucky enough to have one at Wootton Bassett School. How are the reports circulated and used, though?

◆ We need to create communities within which we can hold dialogues about the educational knowledge we are creating and using. There are local groups, there are national groups like the Collaborative Action Research Network and (maybe) the British Educational Research Association. There needs to be co-ordination of these groups, though, on a professional basis. The General Teaching Council is dead, politically speaking. The way ahead lies, it seems to me at the moment, with the embryonic Education Council which Tyrrell Burgess and others have been working on. Through this professional body, we will have a chance to evolve a shared understanding of educational knowledge, and to use it professionally, in a process of dialogue taking place through conferences, meetings, a journal, a newsletter and so on. I'll send you further information; I'd be very interested in your comments and responses.

I'm out of time and space. There are still lots of things I feel I haven't replied to, but I hope this won't be our last contact. Thanks again for taking the trouble to read my paper, and for making such a stimulating reply to it.

Very best wishes

Kevin Eames

CONVERSATION TWO

ALICE OTTO

I am Alice Otto, an educator at Washington University School of Medicine, which is located in the Midwest section of the United States. Having received my education and training in medicine at Washington University, I became involved in the private practice of pediatric anesthesiology in Southern California. I was most fortunate to have received my graduate training at the M.A. level in Curriculum and Instruction from the University of California, Riverside. Upon returning to St. Louis, I continued my educational studies through the opportune meeting and friendship of Professor Lou Smith. My interests are focused in studying the curricular characteristics of graduate medical education. I use a Schwabian conception of curriculum and I am most interested in the examination of the relationship and interplay between teacher, learner, subject matter and milieu in this setting. At present, I am teaching anesthesiology to medical residents and student nurse anesthetists at the Washington University School of Medicine. In 1993 I will be travelling to the University of Tanzania as a visiting professor to examine these components in an educational setting that is much different from that in the United States.

TERESA LEHANE

My parents and family are Irish and I was born in London in 1959. After teacher training in Liverpool (B.Ed. 'Mental Handicap') I saw a TV documentary about the appalling conditions in some hospitals. Eager to change the world, I started nurse training in a large 'Mental Subnormality' hospital. One year of institutionalised chaos later, I left and began teaching in a hospital school. Since then I have taught children aged 2-19 in variously designated special schools. These days, we describe the children as having 'severe learning difficulties', and I have always especially liked working with those children with profound and multiple learning difficulties. In my present job I also masquerade as Deputy Head and recently completed an M.Ed. at Worcester College of Higher Education. My research interest is to try to enhance my own practice and the everyday school experiences of the children at my school and those who work with them.

GRADUATE MEDICAL EDUCATION: ACTION RESEARCH'S OUTER LIMITS

Alice Otto

Problems faced by the teacher in post secondary education appear different in character from those of the elementary and secondary teacher. The learners look different, the subject matter is different, the evaluations are, debatably, of greater consequence, the books are heavier, and the tuition more costly. But the problems of teaching are still centred on the improvement in the quality of the action of teaching. In this sense, the examination of teaching practices in higher education is as amenable to action research as any other educational setting.

Action research is a form of educational enquiry that rests on the following major tenets: (1) The professional is the researcher (Winter, 1989); indeed, outside researchers are not as effective in the methodology of action research (Elliott, 1976). (2) The end result of action research is the deeper understanding of the particular problem in the specific educational setting and the resolution of that problem as a result of the change in action of the researcher-teacher (Winter, 1989; Elliott, 1978; Corey, 1953). Action research studies the social situation of the problem as a whole. As in other methodologies associated with qualitative enquiry, in action research there is an emphasis on understanding the context, including actions, dialogue, and the intentions and interpretations of those involved in these words and actions. Action research is distinct among the qualitative methodologies in that its aims are not only to understand situations, but also to initiate actions that 'improve the quality of action within it [the situation]' (Winter, 1989, p.3).

What follows is an account of a teacher-researcher in graduate medical education in anesthesiology at an American University-Affiliated Hospital. The paper will explain the cycle of action research that was and is being undertaken, the findings which became problematic in the case study, the decisions made regarding these problems and the practical changes in teacher practice. It will include a discussion of the successes and difficulties resulting from those changes.

The action research project grew from the results of another more traditional quantitative investigation that proved unproductive in terms of the statistical significance of the data. The teacher-researcher was an instructor at a university affiliated graduate medical training program in anesthesiology. Along with a colleague at a community based hospital training program, she undertook an examination of the similarities and differences in the two programs. Together they applied correlative statistical methods to the information gained by interviewing the student anesthetist in the two programs. The results of the statistical instrument showed no significant differences in the students' perceptions regarding the value of lectures and the opportunity and availability of personal tutoring in the clinical setting of the operating theaters. Both groups felt the didactic lectures were of some, but only secondary importance to, the clinical teaching. Of greater importance was the frequent comment that the clinical teaching was lacking and the students uniformly desired an improvement in that setting.

The investigators reviewed the notes of the interviews and it became apparent to them that an improvement in clinical teaching practices was universally desired by the students. The student interviews revealed that the students of both programs felt teaching in anesthesiology presents the opportunity for a one-to-one interaction between teacher and learner that is unique in graduate medical education. In anesthesiology, the teacher and learner spent hours together daily, performing anesthetic procedures in the operating theaters. Unlike in other graduate medical specialities that utilised the hierarchical model of senior residents, who teach junior residents and following down the order to intern and medical student, anesthesiology offered the situation that the attending faculty member was juxtapositioned with only one resident for the entire day. During this time the faculty member was responsible for the professional teaching of only one learner, irrespective of his/her level of experience.

Despite the opportunity for this unique teaching situation, the learners stated that this did not occur to their satisfaction. They noted that in other medical specialities (surgery and internal medicine) the faculty spent a greater amount of time with the learners. ('Surgeons take the time in the OR with their residents, but the anesthesia residents can't have the OR time to learn'; no one 'would just sit in the OR [and teach]'; 'The attending [faculty member] is generally absent after the induction'; 'Let's do it this way, good bye'). Additionally, the residents felt that the timing of the teaching that did occur was not conducive to learning and that faculty provided only terse answers to their questions, not in-depth discussion of the underlying medical principles. (The students commented: 'The faculty are waiting for you to ask a question and then they answer. They don't ask'; 'They [faculty] have the knowledge, but you can't get it out of them').

1. Research methods and data collection

The data for this action research project was collected over a nine month period. The problem stated by the students, that of deficiencies in operating room teaching, began to unfold in the winter and spring of 1990. This was the commencement of the traditional interview project and also the time in which I became Chair of the Education Committee. The problems were presented to me in the forms of both formal interviews with open ended questions of the students and informal asides by the residents. I began simply by keeping mental notes of the comments. Within a short time, I began to memo comments and keep a file. I also noted and filed comments from any other members of the department.

The files included not just comments and statements from the students, but also my own reflections on the substance of teaching in graduate medical education. I began gradually to implement changes in my clinical teaching and keep a journal of daily activities. One of the shortcomings, in retrospect, was that the journal contained my thoughts and reasoning and the observed behaviors of my students, but few quoted comments from them.

Over the next six months, I noted daily activities and new problems as they arose. Analysis of the memos and my journal entries provided the data for this report.

2. Analysis of the problematic situation

As the teacher-researcher, I then began the first step in the action research cycle (Elliott, 1976), by examining the problems of teaching in the clinical setting of the operating theater. I reflected on the complexity of this educational setting involving: (1) the teaching of highly specific subject matter; (2) the need for rapid decision making to ensure patient safety; and (3) the necessity of participation of many other professionals in the care of the patient, but not directly involved in the anesthesia educational setting.

3. The subject matter requirements

The subject matter that must be mastered by the anesthesia student is an enormous amount and relatively untouched in medical school. The basics of physiology and pharmacology are given, but the relation to anesthetic management is not. Additionally, the teacher uses the actual anesthetic event to teach. Only two hours per week was spent in a traditional classroom setting compared to the 50 to 60 hours per week teaching in the operating theaters during actual anesthetic procedures. This was compounded by the problem that most OR teaching was anecdotal, based on personal experiences of the anesthetist-teacher, and not formal lessons of pharmacology and physiology. Also, there was very little available time for any other formal lessons in the didactic schedule of the department.

4. Elements of instructional milieu

In the operating theater, the anesthetist-teacher both conducts and teaches his/her student how to conduct an anesthetic using an actual patient. Because of the potency of the anesthetic drugs, their results are rapidly seen and decisions regarding needed changes in management need to be equally as rapid. Again, the teacher must teach his/her student both how to make the correct choices and how to make those decisions rapidly. The third compounding factor in teaching anesthesia in the operating theater is the presence of many other participants; surgeons, nurses, technicians to operate equipment, are necessarily involved in patient care. They all require effective and frequent communication with the anesthetist-teacher for issues of patient safety. The anesthetist-teacher must both answer their needs for information and teach at the same time.

All of these factors make teaching in this setting difficult. This difficulty was reflected in the student anesthetist's comments regarding the lack of clinical teaching in the operating room setting. As a professional educator, I attempted to solve this problem in my own teaching.

5. Cycles of resolution

One of the student's comments was that the faculty member was present at the start of the anesthetic procedure, attempted to teach at that point and then disappeared ('Attending faculty members are generally absent after the induction'; 'Let's do it this way, goodbye'). The induction of anesthesia is an extremely busy and complex event; the student anesthetist is often overwhelmed by the magnitude and rapidity of events that are involved. The student anesthetists made a clear point, that the time of induction of anesthesia is not a time for the student to be open and receptive to learning. ('OR teaching occurs at a time when I'm too busy'; 'Teaching during induction is inappropriate'). Rather he/she would prefer to be taught after the anesthetic is 'coasting along' - in other words, later in the procedure.

In response to that, I changed my teaching practice such that during the induction of the anesthetic, I would perform my duties quietly. I would make note to the student only when I wanted him/her to be particularly aware of some action and allow him/her to observe mine and the patient's responses. This allowed two actions to occur: (1) the student could pay full attention to the events of the anesthetic induction, and (2) the student could gain confidence in his/her abilities at this eventful time. I was not interrupting with comments that were off the cuff and not solidly thought through. This technique was also of use to me as the teacher. It gave me another valuative instrument for my student. I was able to focus on the student's performance, its strengths and deficits, and then offer constructive criticism. We both gained professionally and educatively from this step. Most of my comments at this point involved improvement of the resident's techniques. By not interpreting his/her plan and management, I could see when he/she allowed too much or too little time between the doses of drugs. Too much time between the doses allowed the patient partially to return to consciousness and make reanesthetizing more difficult, while too short an interval caused too great a depression on the heart and blood pressure. Additionally, standing at a distance from the operating table allowed me to examine the positioning of the patient on the table and look for areas of pressure on nerves or potential for injuries.

The institution of this practice led to another problem. If I do not teach at induction of anesthesia (that is, the more traditional time), when do I teach? From the student's comments, I hypothesised that an appropriate time would be at a point when the rush of the induction of anesthesia was completed, the surgeon is occupied with the business at hand, the patient is stable, and my anesthetic drugs are in full effect. I found that it was necessary to set aside a specific time for this to occur. I would review my schedule of cases for the day and set aside a period with each of the students, and then make sure that I was in the operating theater at that time.

I found an important element of this teaching to be some sort of cue that the student could read as 'this is the time to teach'. I used verbal cues ('Let's talk about ... now') and nonverbal ones (I would pull up a chair and sit next to the student). Most other times when I came in to make a supervisory check or solve a specific problem, we both stood and worked at the mechanics of anesthesia. With the use of these cues the student knew that it was time for the teacher/learner interaction. He/she also had the option of saying, 'No, I'm busy now', which is a justified response involving patient care.

Addressing the problem of when to teach brought up more difficult problems of what to teach. I realised that it was much easier to add a quick, off the cuff comment when everyone was busy at induction than to make organised, clear and knowledgeable statements at a designated time. An example of this was merely ordering the resident that he/she should give more of a certain drug to the patient with liver disease ('You need to give more muscle relaxant now') versus explaining the changes that occur in drug distribution with the liver failure. It became necessary that I develop what in essence was a set of lesson plans. This consisted of: (1) a list of topics of interest; (2) underlying basics of pharmacology and physiology; and (3) examples of the relation of these basics to the practice and management of anesthesia.

At first, I allowed the student to dictate the topics discussed. I quickly realised that I was more proficient and had a better understanding of some topics than others. For example, I could readily discuss physiology of the lungs, but the electrical workings of the heart was much harder for me to understand, let alone discuss. I decided to offer the student a choice of selected topics, all of which I felt comfortable with. Then I would allow him/her to choose from there. This was not just for my convenience, but also for the student's benefit. I could teach more fully the topics that I understood more fully.

The second stage in the development of these lesson plans was to ensure that I myself had a complete grasp of the subject matter. The ability to set aside an appropriate time to teach gave rise to the opportunity for discussion between the teacher and the learner. I found these adult learners would question and probe my statements in depth. If they did not understand or had experienced in reading or action something different from my statement, they would initiate a discussion about these controversies. At this point I needed to know the material well. Third, I needed to find appropriate clinical examples of the topics taught. This was not difficult. I chose examples from both books describing anesthetic cases and my own experience.

Again, the cycle of action research became evident. Now that I had solved the problem of a time to teach and the problem of what to teach, the problem of making this relevant to the clinical setting arose. Often this could be accomplished by thinking through the anesthetic management beforehand and selecting appropriate lesson plans. But at times the educational significance of the predesignated lesson was over-shadowed by some more significant, but unanticipated anesthetic event. To let the educational value of this experience go untaught would be a waste, but to teach in an unorganised and incomplete fashion would be a disaster. I had to make a decision on the course of action of my teaching in this regard. I chose at those times to give the student only the information and the thinking process that I used to solve the current problem, in the hope that he/she would learn to recognise the problem and have immediate solutions for that problem. Later, I added a more complete picture of the problem, its etiology and therapy, to the list of my lesson plans. This could be used in a reflective discussion with the student at a later time or be used as another complete lesson plan. In this way I struck a balance between patient safety and well delivered teaching.

These represent the changes that occurred in my own teaching practice. Additionally, as a Chair of the Education Committee for my Department, I was able to institute a number of solutions to the problems of clinical anesthesia teaching at the departmental level. Initially, the Education Committee formed a subcommittee that analysed, recorded and reported to the entire faculty the status of clinical teaching in the operating theaters. Along with the report were suggestions for improving this teaching practice. They included the use of a phone conversation between student and teacher the evening prior to the anesthetic. Here, they discussed the patient and his/her medical problems and their impact on anesthetic management. The purpose of this call was to negotiate a learning contract between the teacher and the learner. Also, there was the formation of small, heterogeneous tutoring groups moderated by interested faculty. Here the participants were given the opportunity to discuss specific anesthetic problems and their management. I used this opportunity fully to teach the serendipitous educative events that occurred in the operating theater. I found that, as part of the process of developing a greater number of the formal lesson plans, I was able to pull up for discussion the appropriate response to the serendipitous event, thereby not losing the 'teachable moment'.

6. *Evaluation of teacher activities*

Evaluation of my teaching activities was an ongoing procedure. The changes were evaluated and modified on a daily basis. I would reflect on the things that went well and the things that went poorly for both myself and the student. Some days I would ask the student to comment on his/her perception of the day. I tried to pick days that the teaching went well and also went poorly. Comments were noted and filed. The residents discussed, for the most part, their own activities and performance rather than evaluating or even discussing mine. A few of the more senior students commented that 'you are the only one attending that lets me do my own case'.

Additionally, there were the departmentally solicited, but anonymous written comments at the end of the year. These comments are traditionally terse. Many of them are one or two lines at the most, using a Likert scale for rating teacher activities. The comments fell into two distinct camps. Fortunately, the positive comments outnumbered the negative ones. The positive ones used familiar superlatives and gracious comments. The negative ones were of intense interest (for example, 'She should spend more time teaching outside of the OR', 'Can be unsafe'). I was not able to identify or further illuminate the reasons behind these comments.

Perhaps the greatest verification of success occurred in the changes in student behavior. Two behaviors became apparent. First, the students without my solicitation began to say, 'Let's talk about ... tomorrow', when we discussed case management the night prior. The number of students that freely addressed this has continually grown. Initially, only the senior students and specifically those with whom I had a personal rapport would initiate this interaction. Of late, more of the junior students, those with whom I have not worked previously and even those with which I do not feel that I have a particular rapport have initiated this comment. Not all of the students do so, but the number is growing.

Additionally, on several instances when the student giving lunch relief would enter the operating theater and see the two of us (the student and myself), the relief student would comment, 'Is this a bad time? Are you teaching?' The finest form of affirmation came when a student told his lunch relief to please come back later, because 'We were discussing ... '.

These episodes evidenced that the changes in teaching practice were viewed by the students as teaching. I am not sure if all were viewed as good teaching, but at least they are seen as teaching. My hopes are that I will be able to improve the quality such that all are episodes of good teaching. But at least there is some teaching occurring in the operating theaters.

CONCLUSIONS

Key points to the discussion of this action research project included:

(1) the acknowledgement of a practical problem of teaching; in this case, teaching clinical anesthesia in the operating theater;
(2) the decisions formulated in the light of the actual problems:
(3) changes in teaching practice;
(4) the cyclic nature of the action research process.

The problems of clinical teaching in anesthesia were examples of 'the practical problems that they [teachers] face in their classrooms' (Elliott, 1976). As Elliott stated, these problems are too complex to be understood from a single standpoint and must be approached in the intact setting to analyse and propose solutions. The problem of clinical teaching in anesthesia was presented to me by students. It was not a theoretical hypothesis that I arbitrarily and artificially operationalised, then proceeded to find a measuring instrument that would give numbers and statistical significance to the artifical variables of this educational setting. The evaluation of the students' stated needs for better clinical teaching in the operating theaters, and the problem of when and how to accomplish this, were real problems in my teaching.

This process further reflected elements of action research that are responsible for the 'action' component of the name: (1) the element of actual changes that are made in the practice of teaching (Winter, 1989), and (2) the cyclic nature of action research. The decisions that I made were fulfilled in actual and real changes made in my teaching practice. Unlike the hypothesis-testing researcher, action research gave me readily usable information to be incorporated into my practice. Additionally, each of the steps of change led to another more complex question that I needed to resolve. Winter (1989) addressed this point when speaking of the spiralling relation between the analysis of the research problem and solution leading to new problems. I found this true and would add that with an increased understanding of the problem, that each successive question becomes more complex. Each successive question required more information to resolve and a more difficult solution. Neither Elliott nor Winter addressed the fact that the spiral is of ever increasing depth and complexity. This is a finding that was true for my research.

Additionally, this project illustrated well another principle of action research, that of viewing the situation as a whole and in a practical context. Lewin (1951) points out that field theory does not pick out the isolated event, but rather views the situation as a whole. The importance of this was made clear to me, when I contrasted this action research project with a project that the Education Committee had undertaken in the recent past. As a body, the Education Committee within the department had also realised the inadequacy of teaching in the operating theaters. We had decided to appoint a subcommittee to study and solve the problem. The subcommittee met and arrived at grand schemes of what was to happen in the operating theaters. Their recommendations were not grounded in the realities of the operating theaters, the appropriate time to teach, the need for interaction with other members of the operating team, and management of serendipitous educative events. Their recommendations were difficult to implement because of their abstractness. The research of the committee became more a written exercise than a change in action.

This account is of the curricular changes that occurred as a result of the action research process within a department of graduate medical education in anesthesiology. On the individual level, changes were made in my own understanding of the teaching practice. From my research, I arrived at the following theories:

(1) The vast distribution of the educational time for the anesthesia resident is spent in the operating theater, and the corresponding amount of teaching should occur there also. The limited amount of time spent in formal didactic sessions could not possibly cover the amount of subject matter to be mastered.

(2) Even though the amount of time spent in the OR is great, the timing of the teaching is specific. There are and there are not times to teach and learn, and the teacher must distinguish between the two. Requirements for an appropriate time to learn are stricter than for the time to teach. The teacher must allow the learner to be comfortable with the situation and able to attend to the teaching with his/her whole self. One can surely offer instruction and information at any time, but if the learner is occupied (and justifiably so with matters of patient wellbeing) then the process of teaching and learning did not occur. This is in distinction to the educational setting in which the only participants are the teacher and the learner. In graduate medical education, there is a third and critical participant - the patient. It was unrealistic and unsafe to demand that the learner remove his/her attention from the patient at a critical time, for the sole benefit of the teacher's ease of teaching.

(3) I found that the subject matter to be taught needed to be formally organised and clearly understood by the teacher for effective teaching.

The changes in my action of teaching that were undertaken by my understanding of these problems included:

(a) Choosing a time and setting that was conductive to both teaching and learning, one outside the hectic demands of some portions of anesthetic management.
(b) Choosing topics that I had a clear understanding of, underlying principles of pharmacology and physiology.
(c) Managing unexpected but clinically significant events in an educative manner.

A key element to the use of action research is that of reflection (Winter, 1989; McKernan, 1991). Reflection is used to develop an understanding of the problem and the evaluation of the successes of the solutions. In this respect, reflection is invaluable to the researcher. Another element of reflection needs to be added to the process of action research, that is, of reflection on past experiences, those past experiences of both the researcher and other education researchers dealing with similar problems. Few reports of action research have added the context of past experience to their conclusions. Admittedly, those experiences of others are not necessary for action research, but they add depth and new perspectives to our understanding of a problem. Without them, action research is forever reinventing the educational wheel. Elliott (1976) spoke to the use of pre-existing theory to guide and change teacher practices. Elliott did not have a problem with the use of theory to change practice, but rather he objected to the isolation of theory from matters of practice. He proposed that established theory be used as an instrument to allow more thorough self-reflection by the teacher. '[Curriculum] Reformers fail to realise that fundamental changes in classroom practice can only be brought about if the teachers become conscious of the theories which guide their practice and are able to reflect critically about them' (Elliott, 1976, p.2).

Elliott further states that the 'curriculum reform movement has had a largely missed opportunity to involve teachers in the process of theory development' (ibid, p.2). Action research is one vehicle in which teachers can both test pre-existing theory and develop new.

A further understanding of this research problem was gained by the re-examination of John Dewey's conception of the role of teacher and use of subject matter (Dewey, 1902). (Please note: This is the beginning of my re-examination of Dewey. The following is an initial attempt at understanding curriculum research from this stance. I think that Dewey and action research can be linked, and I am investigating the ways.) Dewey, in 'The Child and the Curriculum', called for action in teaching as a means of improvement of the activity of teaching. This parallels the perceived need for problem resolution that initiates the action research cycle.

Dewey addressed the need to organize lessons with underlying principles of the subject matter. I found this speaks to the problem of using organized plans instead of off the cuff remarks. Dewey stated that putting forth facts without substantiation and explanation is an uneducative manoeuvre. 'Now, any fact, whether of arithmetic, or geography or grammar, which is not led up to and out of something which has previously occupied a significant position in the child's life for its own sake is forced into this position. It is not a reality, but just a sign of the reality which might be experienced if certain conditions are fulfilled. But the abrupt presentation of the facts as something known by others and requiring only to be studied and learned by the child, rules out the conditions of fulfilment. It condemns the fact to be a hieroglyph: it would mean something if one only had the key. The clue being lacking, it remains an idle curiosity, to fret and obstruct the mind, a dead weight to burden it.' (Dewey, 1902, p.25).

This certainly was the case of the off the cuff remarks at induction of anesthesia. The exhortation and orders were mere facts and without connection to 'something which has previously occupied a significant position in the child's [student's] life', such as pharmacology, physiology, or anatomy. Merely offering facts to the learner resulted in their memorizing many disjointed algorithms but no basis to interpret or act on new problems in their practice.

Dewey spoke well to the role of teacher in this study. He stated that the role of teacher is one of guidance. The teacher was to choose subject matter and translate it to the terms of the learner. 'He is concerned with the subject matter of science as representing a given stage and phase of development of experience. ... Hence, what concerns him, as a teacher, is the way in which the subject may become part of the experience ... how his own knowledge of the subject matter may assist in interpreting the child's needs and doings and determine the medium in which the child is to be placed in order that his growth may be properly directed' (Dewey, 1902, p.23). Dewey also noted that to accomplish this the teacher must determine the environment of the learner and thereby direct the situation. This is analogous to my choice of determining the appropriate timing of instruction. If I merely offered information at the usual time of induction of anesthesia, without consideration for the environment of the situation, the educative value of the instruction was severely diminished. Additionally, Dewey addressed not only timing but also level of instruction and abstraction. I found this also to be true in the construction of my lesson plans. Some of the residents, regardless of the level of experience, were able to understand concepts at a deeper level of abstraction and correlation. Some of the students had special needs: understanding and overcoming a particular deficit required me to adapt my lesson plans accordingly.

The role of guidance for Dewey is paramount. Without guidance from the teacher, experience is out of context. The learner is left 'to spin new truths of nature' (Dewey, 1902, p.18) in explanation of the phenomenon experienced. I found this particularly true in the setting of graduate medical education. Without the guidance of the faculty, the students constructed the medical reality of the situation on the basis of their limited knowledge. A frequent resident shortcoming, cited by the faculty, was that the residents 'made up' pharmacology and physiology to suit the setting. I found this to be true, but more the result of faculty lack of guidance in the art of relating experience to past knowledge.

Dewey obviously does not address the particulars of graduate medical education, but I feel that he speaks to my philosophical values that ultimately directed my course of action as a result of this research.

References

Corey, S.M., *Action Research to Improve School Practices* (New York, Teachers' College, Columbia University, 1953).

Dewey, J., *The Child and the Curriculum; The School and Society* (Chicago: The University of Chicago Press, 1902).

Elliott, J., 'Developing hypotheses about classrooms from teachers' practical constructs: an account of the work of the Ford Teaching Project': a Paper presented at the Annual Meeting, American Educational Research Association, San Francisco, California (April 19-23, 1976).

Elliott, J., 'What is action research?': a paper presented at the CARN Conference, Wolfson Court, Cambridge (7-9 July, 1978).

Elliott, J., 'Educational theory, practical philosophy and action research' in British Journal of Educational Studies, 35(2): 149-169 (1987).

Lewin, K., *Field Theory in Social Science* (New York: Harper & Row, 1951).

McKernan, J. *Curriculum Action Research* (Kogan Page, 1991).

Winter, R., *Learning From Experience: Principles and Practice in Action Research* (London: The Falmer Press, 1989).

WHAT I WOULD LIKE TO DISCUSS WITH YOU

Teresa Lehane

I would like to attempt to review your paper in the same way that we might review a work by Shakespeare, as opposed to the way current books and articles are often reviewed in the press. Just like looking critically and reflectively at one's own professional practice, the former does not 'criticise' or weigh negative and positive in the balance in any quantitative sense. Instead, it seeks to try to understand what the writer is feeling and saying, pointing up threads, themes and tensions and asking more questions. I feel this is potentially a most valuable exercise but in my case a very tentative one, not least because it is impossible for anyone fully to understand another's personal and professional identity. I find the process of trying, however, quite compelling.

A striking duality permeates your writing. Yes, it is a celebration of the 'equivalence' of the work of action researchers because, whatever the educational context, whether the desks are large, small or non-existent, we all focus on improving the quality of our teaching. Nevertheless, while you successfully bring the non-specialist into the world of anaesthesia with refreshingly lucid writing, you are right to make us hold on to the certainty that your 'classroom' differs in that a patient's very life is suspended in the hands of you and your students.

I find your portrayal shows many similarities between your world (American graduate medical education) and mine (U.K. special school). The need to teach a coherent (often pre-specified) curriculum while retaining the capacity to relate to students' individual needs and experience, and to use serendipitous events as 'teachable moments', is very familiar. You chronicle the changes you are making in response to your own dissatisfaction and that of your students to the timing, content and style of your teaching. Clearly you speak the same language as action researchers in other fields in showing that you contend with conflicting values—for example, between the requirements of teaching and the demand for patient safety.

Your experience of the sub-committee which 'met and arrived at grand schemes of what was to happen in the operating theatres', which 'were not grounded in the realities', and which largely remained as a written exercise rather than change in action, clearly strike a chord with the grand-scale British and American curriculum projects of the 1960s and 70s and the watershed British curriculum legislation of the 1980s and 90s. Your writing is a significant addition to my list of 'frontline researchers' who help grant permission to pursue a viable alternative—to research what I really feel is important. My first 'specimen' was the paper by Magdalene Lampert (1985) which deals with organization of seating in her elementary classroom. Her rigorous and sophisticated analysis shows that an issue which appears minor to outsiders is of considerable importance to the practitioner and is far from simple to solve. On the contrary, it highlights contradictions within her own professional values, the nature of unsolvable problems and an awareness of the teacher as a dilemma manager. You, too, have the integrity to write about when is the best time to talk with the student, whether it helps to pull up a chair to sit next to the student, whether to make a 'heat of the moment' comment during induction of anaesthesia or to talk with greater clarity when the student is more relaxed. I call this the 'nitty gritty', and I believe most 'frontliners' would know what I mean, and value this above more ostentatious writing. I feel we live in a hostile climate and that therefore each such honest story of professional improvement is enormously valuable.

The differences between your work and that of others are also most educative. On page 33 you say, ' ... I had solved the problem of a time to teach and the problem of what to teach ... '. The difference between this confidence and my own confusion is interesting. Clearly there are far more absolute standards in medicine than in children's schooling. If you teach your student an incorrect drug dosage your patient will surely die, while if I make errors in planning a lesson it will simply not be a particularly good lesson. Your subject matter is more quantifiable and more sensitive to objective scrutiny. Nevertheless, are there questions which might be posed about it? For example, is the curriculum able to address the patient's perspectives on all aspects of anaesthesia, including long-term and social effects? It might be said that this is simply schoolroom education contemplating its own navel in a way which is an unaffordable luxury for operating room education. Nevertheless, you have gone far in peeling back many of the layers of custom and familiarity of medical training - perhaps just some more to look at too?

I would be interested to hear more of the continuing dialogue between you and your students as you change your way of working as well as the relationships you all have with the operating team as a whole - your complex social setting. Are there any doubts, 'hiccups'

Conversation Two 43

or disasters along the way? I would be interested also to have insight into the political dimensions of your work, as this has become essential to my personal attempts to unravel my own practice. Why are things so tight at the time of inducing the anaesthesia? Is it ideal to spend two hours per week in traditional classroom settings compared to 50 to 60 hours per week teaching in the operating theatres during anaesthetic procedures? If you and your student are also the only anaesthetists for the operating team, is this the ideal way to proceed or simply the way that things are done? How do your students feel by the sixtieth hour of learning of the week? I find it difficult and painful to raise similar issues which impinge on my own practice - issues of resources and staffing as well as the implications for personal practice of working within a system which segregates children with learning difficulties from their peers. The feeling of powerlessness is overwhelming and yet it feels a little less so once I attempt to look at it with 'strangers' eyes' and not proceed with the status quo solely as a 'given'.

A political perspective would also be helpful when reading about your personal professional philosophy. You thoughtfully espouse Dewey's argument that 'any fact ... whether of arithmetic, or geography, or grammar, which is not led up to and out of something which has previously occupied a significant position in the child's life for its own sake ... is not a reality ... and the abrupt presentation of the facts as something known by others and requiring only to be studied and learned by the child, rules out the conditions of fulfilment'. Are you encouraged to develop your personal philosophy in this way? In the U.K., the Secretary of State for Education is currently demanding a return to a whole class, subject-centred, didactic teaching, presumably because he sees it as 'plain old-fashioned common sense' (John Patten in *The Guardian,* 19 January, 1993) regardless of individual teachers' views. It would be good to develop the work on Dewey (and perhaps of other theorists) in relation to your own personal and professional theories - and perhaps in relation to the social and political aspects of your work.

AND IN REPLY

Alice Otto

I was most interested in your comments, Teresa, regarding the work that I have submitted. After reading your comments, I had the impression that 'you know who I am'. Your commentary discussed both my philosophy of medical education, and views of the current status of curriculum in graduate medical education.

My curricular perspective has been informed by the works of Schwab, Dewey and Schön. As a conception of curriculum, I use an interactive model similar to that of Schwab. Curriculum is the interaction between teacher and learner over subject matter in a specified milieu. I am not as constrained as Schwab. I feel all interactions constitute curriculum, rather than just those 'successfully conveyed to students, by committed teachers, using appropriate materials and actions of legitimated bodies of knowledge, skill, taste and propensity to act and react, which are chosen for instruction after serious reflection.' (Schwab, 1983). I am deeply interested in examining the breadth of curricular experiences in graduate medical education. Through the paradigm of qualitative inquiry, and action research in particular, I am able to view graduate medical education as a complex social setting and examine the influence of all parts on the whole. Schwab is constrained by a positive analysis of educational settings. Because of his basis in traditional positivity, his conceptualization can only be identified by the statistically significant and better solution to a chain of isolated questions.

The conception of curriculum that I employ is additionally informed by the works of Dewey and Schön. Both of these authors address values, individual and societal, in the educational experience. From a qualitative tradition, it becomes essential to examine the political and social influences on the milieu of medical education. Presently, in the United States, medical enterprise and education are influenced heavily by proposed governmental changes in methods of health care delivery. Dewey proposes a type of socialist democracy which is in many ways similar to the health care delivery systems proposed.

Schön's contribution of reflective practice brings into examination the Deweyian proposals of personal views of teaching and medical education. Reflective practice has enabled me to move my social values of medical education to the teaching arena on a day-to-day basis.

The second topic that your comments capture is the present milieu of graduate medical education. You comment on the apprenticeship model that is omnipresent in graduate medical education. Here, long hours are spent learning a specialized trade from a master craftsman on a one-to-one basis, in a controlled and exclusive setting. The long hours in the operating room represent the rite of passage into the profession. This strong tradition must be taken into account when any analysis of curriculum is undertaken. One of the 'disasters' in my change to operating room teaching was reflected in the comments of a student: 'Dr. Otto is an outstanding teacher; education outside the operating room is her fate.' I feel that my failure lies in the fact that I did not recognize the power of the apprenticeship and the master craftsman model of the teacher who imparts all knowledge and information. Rather I had a negotiated knowledge base with the student. I now have incorporated my role as master craftsman to readily identifiable behaviours and propensities to act, still negotiating subject matter and shared knowledge, but respecting the importance of the social milieu.

CONVERSATION THREE

COLIN HENRY

I am a Senior Lecturer in the School of Curriculum and Administrative Studies, in the Faculty of Education, Deakin University, Geelong. I worked as a primary and secondary school teacher in Australia and Canada before commencing university teaching in the late 1980s. My beyond-work interests revolve around my wife and four grown-up children, despite the fact that all of them are unrelenting in their critique of my taste in shirts, my slow driving and my conviction that *The Missouri Breaks* is the greatest film ever made. I am keen on reading, riding and Western flicks, and spend a good bit of my spare time growing native plants and developing the 25 acres the family has on the outskirts of Geelong.

BRIDGET SOMEKH

I have been a member of CARN since 1979 and Co-ordinator since 1987. I have a wide range of experience of action research. My early work was as a teacher researching children's learning and institutional development in the school where I was Head of the English department. Since moving to work at the Centre for Applied Research in Education, at the University of East Anglia, I have co-ordinated two major action research projects looking at possible ways of using Information Technology to support learning: the Pupil Autonomy in Learning with Microcomputers Project (PALM) and the Initial Teacher Education and New Technology Project (INTENT). I am interested in computers because of the intense emotions they tend to arouse in both teachers and students, and their apparent capacity to disturb the established patterns of classroom practice - I see these as necessary, but by no means sufficient, conditions for enabling change. I have edited several CARN publications and am co-author, with Herbert Altrichter and Peter Posch, of *Teachers Investigate Their Work*, published by Routledge in 1993.

McDONALD'S, REPUBLICANISM AND BOTHAM'S EARLY DEPARTURE: DEMOCRATIC EDUCATION FOR A CHANGE?

Colin Henry

When John Mortimer's wise, but often world-weary, character Horace Rumpole is moved to direct his gaze beyond the exigencies of the Old Bailey and reflect more philosophically on legal practice, he is known to observe that the golden thread running through the British legal system is the presumption of innocence. Rumpole's virtue is that he understands the difference between legal traditions which matter and those which do not and, moreover, that he is conscious of the connection between his own everyday work at the bar and the maintenance of valued legal practices and institutions. What endears Rumpole to us, most of all, is that his legal practice is guided by ethical principles even at some cost to his professional standing, his income and his career.

Perhaps, if we were to take Rumpole's lead, it is possible to argue that there is also a golden thread which runs through educational action research; that it is the presumption of collective autonomy; and that, in the absence of a commitment to collective autonomy, the fabric of action research unravels and falls apart. We might also find that although action research sits uncomfortably with the current trend towards educational uniformity and standardisation, it simultaneously is a means of transforming the relationship between academic researchers and other practitioners (such as teachers or workplace educators), and of defending educational and social traditions worth fighting for (Fullan, 1991).

Collective autonomy and the democratisation of social relations

The notion of 'collective autonomy' in the context of educational practice implies, as I understand it, that teachers, students, parents, workplace educators, workers, consultants, academics and others involved in educational activities (such as a school review, a staff development program or a curriculum improvement project) are capable both of identifying educational values and priorities and acting together to realise those values and priorities. Put another way, collective autonomy means individual teachers (or workplace educators) and groups of teachers (or workplace educators), among others, taking responsibility for what is happening to them, even in *the midst of a dependency-creating culture.*

Collective autonomy, in this sense, has a good deal in common with many well-known definitions of participatory democracy. It has much in common, for instance, with the concept of socialist democracy and the aim of democratising social relations that is a consistent theme in Raymond Williams' writings (Rizvi, 1989). Williams (1983) had a straightforward view of the theory and practice of democracy:

In any event the principle is, and the practice should be, that all decisions should be taken by those who are directly concerned with them (p.124).

As Williams saw it, democracy meant self-management, that is, 'ordinary' people having the power and resources they need to manage their own affairs. Concrete practices such as the devolution of authority to people working in schools (and other workplaces), self-governing schools (and other work sites), and parent participation in school-based decision making (or worker participation in shop- or office-based decision making), exemplified what Williams saw as democracy in action.

In the United States., democracy has been similarly conceptualised by Hanna Pitken and Sara Shumer (Pitken and Shumer, 1982):

The basic idea (of democracy) is simple: people can and should govern themselves. They do not need specially bred or annointed leaders, nor a special caste or class to run their affairs. Everyone has the capacity for autonomy, even quite ordinary people - the uneducated, the poor, housewives, laborers, peasants, the outsiders and castoffs of society. Each is capable not merely of self-control, of privately taking control of his life, but also of self-government, of sharing in the deliberate shaping of their common life. Exercising this capacity is prerequisite both to the freedom and self-development of each, and to the freedom and justness of the community (p.43).

In Australia, increasing evidence of injustice and distress resulting from eight years of rational (?) economics-driven politics (Manne, 1992) has provided a fresh perspective on the possibilities of participatory democracy. Donald Horne (1992), for example, has argued that in coming to grips with our economic problems,

We should take our citizens into the discussion and we should have more emphasis on a case by case analysis, recognising that different

cases might demand different actions, and might not be resolved by just following a couple of simple ideological rules.

In other words, instead of being dogmatic, why not raise discussion, have a think, and try to make it an intelligent public issue? We are supposed to be a democracy. We might start acting like one, instead of speaking of the citizens as if they were only manipulable voters (p.11).

Now, what do these democratic principles mean for action research?

In schools, they mean that educational action research projects based on democratic principles, or the presumption of collective autonomy, will begin by taking teachers, parents, students and other members of school communities into the discussion of what should be done about particular educational issues (such as improving respect for human rights in and through schools, evaluating and reporting children's progress, or creating more authentic links between schools and their communities).

In other work sites, educational action research projects based on democratic principles, or the presumption of collective autonomy, will begin by taking workplace educators, workers, unionists, and others affected by the work into the discussion of what should be done about particular educational issues (such as improving staff development programs in hospitals, upgrading educational programs designed to improve workplace safety in refineries, and creating additional opportunities for existing staff to qualify for more senior secretarial positions in co-operative enterprises).

Such action research projects will be guided by the principle, and characterised by the practice, that all decisions taken during the course of the project are taken by those who are directly concerned with them. When they aspire to self-management, action research projects are undermined by 'expert' direction, bureaucratic control, authoritarian relationships and other policies and practices that constitute the **denial of democracy in everyday life** (Shor, 1980, p.71). Action researchers can be expected to reject hierarchical relationships between academic researchers, on the one hand, and teachers, parents, students, workplace educators, workers, and unionists, on the other, on the grounds that such policies and practices are likely to be inconsistent with the distinctive principle of **maximum self-management** (Williams, 1983, p.125). They can also be expected to steer clear of projects designed to sustain authoritarian practices, oppose participatory decision making processes, and implement centralised directives designed to standardise school curricula or training programs, on similar grounds.

Collective autonomy in the history and literature of action research

The claim that collective autonomy, or the democratisation of social life, is the golden thread which runs through at least certain traditions of action research, can be justified by referring to a substantial history and literature. Among those for whom group deliberation, self-management, self-organisation, and collective work were prominent features of action were John Collier (1945), Sol Tax and Lisa Peattie (1960), and Abraham Shumsky (1956). Shumsky, for example, found the rationale for action research in its democratic methods and co-operative impulse:

An action research movement is potentially a grass roots approach to the solution of community problems. It means activating the social and spiritual life of the community in a continuous search for self-improvement. It means providing a social setting where people can work together, dream together of a better community, and try to translate their dreams into the language of action and evaluation (p.181).

More recently, in the writing of John Gaventa, Myles Horton's successor at the Highlander Centre, we find evidence that Highlander's democratic tradition lives on. For Gaventa, as for Horton, the case for action research hinges on the claim that action research represents a practical means by which community development can be democratised (a means by which large numbers of 'ordinary' people can be enabled to participate in the development of their communities). Gaventa summarises the case for participatory action research by arguing:

Genuine popular participation in the production of knowledge has implications, of course, not only for the realisation of classical notions of democracy but also for the body of knowledge which will be produced. By altering who controls knowledge, what knowledge is produced, and indeed, the very definition of what constitutes knowledge may also change. For example, given the chance to participate in the production of knowledge about products, not just the production of products, the Lucas workers (in a British arms factory which was threatened with closure) chose to develop plans that met basic social needs, not that served as instruments of war. Given the opportunity to define the reasons for poverty through self-analysis, the participants in the Appalachian Land Ownership Study gave a very different set of reasons than had been developed by mainstream social scientists. The vision and view of the world that is produced by the many in their interests will be vastly different than that produced by the few. The believer in

democracy must also have faith that this participatory knowledge of tomorrow will be more human, rational and liberating than the dominating knowledge of today (Gaventa, 1985, p.51).

More recently still, we find the same line running through one of the clearest and most accessible illustrations of the case for participatory action research (and against conventional social research) currently available. The belief that participatory action research produces more human, rational and liberating knowledge than conventional social research, is substantiated by the case developed in South America by the Colombian academic and activist, Orlando Fals Borda (1979; 1987; 1988; 1989; 1990; 1991; forthcoming). This argument is so compelling that you might permit me to discuss it at some length.

Fals Borda's case for participatory action social science is compelling, accessible and engaging, I have found, principally because it appears within the context of an autobiographical account of a successful academic's personal reasons for rejecting orthodox social research and participating in a recent history of community development and political reform. The personal and professional consequences of Fals Borda's rejecting the conventional paradigm of social science were considerable. Two principal effects were his resignation from the prestigious post of Dean and Professor in the National University of Colombia (Bogota) in 1970 and his return to the northern region of the country where he had been raised. There he worked for twenty years with tenant farmers and indigenous people on land reform and community development projects involving participatory action research.

Fals Borda explains his decision to leave the university as a personal response to four crucial intellectual and moral dilemmas he found impossible to resolve while continuing to work within the academy. First, the irrelevance of academic social science to Colombia's pressing social problems; second, continued adherence on the part of academics to the discredited logic of value-free social science; third, the unethical practice of researchers treating other people as objects of social scientific research; and fourth, the academy's arrogant claim to be the sole source of reliable social knowledge.

The first feature of academic life Orlando Fals Borda believed jeopardised his personal and professional integrity was the expectation that he would continue to work within the university, although its intellectual agenda lacked any serious pertinence to Colombia's political, economic and social distress. In his own words, the existential and intellectual problems he found difficult to live with:

> *started with the mortifying discovery that my University, in its actual condition, could not understand adequately the ever-present theory/ practice dialectics. Like many other such institutions, it remained in an ivory tower learning by rote without relating to surrounding social and cultural realities* (Fals Borda, forthcoming, P.1).

Fals Borda traces the institutional shortcomings of the university, and the intellectual dilemmas he experienced as a result of those shortcomings, to pervasive cultural problems deeply rooted in the class divisions of Colombian society. He argues that it was impossible to transform conventional social science into a means of stimulating political action and structural change in the country,

> *because it had been conceived (in Colombia) in terms of the class and power interests of the dominant bourgeoisie. It could not be expected to render its own death blows* (Fals Borda, 1979, p.40).

Thus, a second dilemma Fals Borda found unable to resolve while continuing to work within the university was the tension between tacitly subscribing to the dominant view that scientific research is a technical activity free from responsibility for its social effects while, at the same time, understanding the destruction and social misery frequently caused by the application of scientific research, including social scientific research, to human affairs. The university, he observed, had fallen

> *victim to the fatal belief of science with a life of its own, a notion which I was already connecting with Oppenheimer's denouncement of the atomic bomb* (ibid, p.1).

While he was aware that researchers working within the Newtonian and Cartesian tradition of science (with its emphasis on technical rationality) might continue to convince themselves that commitment to ethical values was inconsistent with 'proper' scientific research, Fals Borda refused to live with such discredited logic. On the contrary, he was convinced that *all interpretations of reality are conditioned by class interests* (Fals Borda, 1979, p.48) and that social research has more frequently been used as an instrument of oppression than of liberation.

A third ethical/intellectual dilemma Fals Borda felt obliged to deal with was the tension between respecting human person-ality and dignity while working within an institution where the conventional social scientific practice of researchers treating other people as if they were no more than passive objects of scientific investigations (mere things to be studied and exploited) was regarded as an unproblematic matter. Conscious *of the problem that individuals and communities frequently become the victims of unilateral scientific exploitation* (Fals Borda, 1979, p.36) in social scientific investigations, Fals Borda,

> *as a social scientist, found increasing difficulty in Spencer's organic analogy or in Durkheim's principles for interpreting social processes and actions as 'facts' or 'things'* (Fals Borda, forthcoming, p.2).

A fourth dilemma for Fals Borda was the presupposition, widespread within the university, of a division of labour between 'ordinary' people and academics in the production of knowledge. Coupled with the presupposition that academics are the subjects of social research (those who conduct research) and 'ordinary' people its objects (those on whom research is done) there was the presumption that academic research is the sole source of reliable knowledge and research the exclusive domain of the university. Hence, the university considered itself, and was widely considered to be, the only source of reliable knowledge. Fals Borda perceived the arrogance of these claims and recognised the need for a very different view of research and researcher, including a very different view of the respective research capabilities of academics and 'ordinary' people:

> *This polemics today is obsolete but in the 1970s it was heretical to preach horizontal relationships in the research adventure even in professional life. It became clear to me however that sociological investigation should not be autistic but a rite of communion between thinking and acting human beings, the researcher and the researched. The usual formality and prophylaxis of academic institutions had to be discarded and replaced by some sort of down to dirt collectivisation in the search for knowledge. This attitude I called vivencia or life experience [Erlebnis]* (ibid, p.2).

The realisation that the social theory normally produced by Colombian academics was irrelevant to the country's pressing social problems; that it was no longer plausible to believe that the value of social scientific research could be divorced from questions of ethical action and moral responsibility; that it was simply wrong to do research on people rather than with and for them; and that knowledge could and was produced by 'ordinary' people as well as academics; added up to a devastating critique of conventional social research. The case against academic sociology, in particular, and conventional social science, in general, convinced Fals Borda that the dominant view of social science within the universities of Colombia was *a major obstacle to changing the ugly reality fraught with violence* (ibid, p.4) that characterised the daily life of most Colombians. As a consequence of the inadequacies of conventional social research, he believed it was necessary to

> *work with a different concept of science more ethical and pertinent to the daily vicissitudes of the common people which would place me on the side of peace and progress, not death and destruction* (ibid, p.1).

The results of twenty years of active service in the front-lines of the struggle for land reform in northern Colombia illustrate what Orlando Fals Borda meant by 'more ethical and pertinent social research'. He admits to *agonising problems of work conception* (Fals Borda, 1979, p.33), to *failures, misunderstandings and polemics, and to work which was not always coherent and suffered from inevitable errors* (ibid, P.34). Nevertheless, he concludes that eventually the work he conducted in collaboration with his colleagues demonstrated to them the potential of participatory action research and its capacity to stimulate political and social reform through the development of alternative social movements and the exercise of people's collective power. The results of involving the poor, dispossessed and oppressed in social study and scientific research and, above all, the 'political clout' that poor and oppressed people were able to wield as a consequence of such study (through being well informed when confronting opponents in court cases over land claims, for example) led Fals Borda to draw a remarkable conclusion about the potential of participatory action research. Through participatory action research, he argues, it was possible to unleash a chain reaction of human energy, social emancipation and political transformation:

> *The evidence that it is possible to produce serious responsible knowledge apt to accumulate through group vivencias (shared life experience) and symmetrical information exchange became so exhilarating for me and the colleagues who accompanied me, that we started to compare the break-up of the subject/object relation in sociology with the fission of the atom in physics. ... We finally came to see participation as a break-up of the relationship of submission, exploitation or oppression between subjects and objects in most expressions of daily life. Finally, as our social commitment increased, the resulting participatory research concept opened the gate to the more ambitious idea of participatory democracy. This was premonitory for further work with political implications: in fact, participatory democracy became a central premise for Colombia's first Constituent Assembly in one hundred years for which I was nominated and elected in December 1990* (ibid, P.3).

As a consequence of this experience of participatory action research, Fals Borda feels justified in concluding that participatory action research may represent a new paradigm in the social sciences.

Summarising the Fals Borda case for participatory action research suggests such an alternative paradigm in which:

(i) the idea that social research is an end in itself, divorced from its contribution to ethical, political and social action, gives way to a conception of social research whose purpose is to inform emancipatory social action in the interest of democratic social and political transformation. Thus, respectable social research is no longer understood as a value-free activity or *as science without ethical qualms* (ibid. p.2). Justifiable social research is, then, social research which has an explicit ethical orientation, *motivated by knowing and acting with a vision of a better world especially for the underprivileged* (ibid. p.4).

(ii) the idea that social research is validated by its logical sophistication gives way to the view that *results are assessed in real life* (Fals Borda, 1989, p.4), that is, by evaluating the effects social research has on concrete social and political transformation;

(iii) the view that it is unproblematic to treat 'ordinary people' as the passive objects of social research is replaced by the view that ordinary people should be regarded as producers of scientific knowledge and as beneficiaries; and

(iv) the presumption that universities and other elite institutions are the sole source of reliable knowledge yields to the claim that reliable knowledge and wisdom is also to be found among 'ordinary' people and created by them, even though popular knowledge and wisdom is often neglected or even despised by academics and elite groups in general.

Fals Borda recognises the irony of calling such a view (metatheory) of social science a 'new' paradigm. His knowledge of the history and philosophy of social science is such that it enables him to locate critical social science within a long intellectual tradition that encompasses not only the work of Saint-Simon, Comte, and Bacon, but also Marx, Gramsci and the members of the Frankfurt School. In a passage that is reminiscent of the work of Alasdair McIntyre in its historical sophistication (Fals Borda, 1981), Orlando Fals Borda recalls a tradition of social research which always included

> *positive methods and philosophies for sociopolitical change which later scholars disregarded for the sake of Cartesian objectivity* (ibid, P.1).

It is important to note that, although he is conscious of his debt to Marx and certain Marxists, Orlando Fals Borda is explicitly critical of hard-line Marxism. He is opposed to the tyranny of the left as well as that of the right, and is critical (in the sense of finding fault with) authoritarian manifestations of Marxism. Fals Borda observes that an important lesson in political science that he learned from bitter experience of hard-line leftists and their tactics in the Colombian countryside, was that *the classical Lukacsian-Leninist concept of a vanguard party* (ibid, p.5) had to be substantially modified if it was to be a force for positive political and social change. By that he means that liberation movements which employ oppression and repression as their political strategy are bound to fail through self-contradiction. Such instrumental strategies are, therefore, neither a satisfactory way of achieving social revolution nor of creating participatory democracy. Fals Borda's experience causes him to believe that there are more constructive and effective approaches to social and cultural transformation. In summary, he defines these approaches as political processes which are *inspired by tolerance, altruism and respect for life and diversity as most peoples wanted it* (ibid. p.5).

Finding better ways of doing educational research

It is not difficult to find the same critique (or, at least, elements of the critique) directed by Fals Borda at conventional social research in the literature on educational action research (see, for example, Corey, 1949; Klafki, 1975; Stenhouse, 1975). There, too, we find the claim that most conventional educational research has little relevance to pressing educational problems, including those experienced by people in and around schools and other work sites; that it is no longer possible to pretend that educational research is value-neutral and without positive consequences for this social group and negative consequences for another; that there is something plainly objectionable about academics treating teachers, students, workplace educators, workers and others as mere objects of their research studies; and that only an insufferable arrogance could lead members of university faculties of education to believe that all there is worth knowing about education and training is the product of their research. The emphasis Stephen Corey (1949) placed on co-operation between curriculum researchers engaged in fundamental research and those engaged in action research, might serve to illustrate the point that the limitations of conventional educational research are well rehearsed in the action research literature:

I would like to emphasise this observation that research, particularly as it pertains to improvement of the curriculum, will be more influential when it is co-operative action research. If, for example, we want to develop experimentally a program of General Education for a high school, our investigation must take into account the ideas and experiences and expectations of pupils, teachers, administrators, parents and other lay adults, all of whom will influence and will be influenced by the program. Unless we do this, we are learning less about General Education and the factors influencing it than we might otherwise. This does not mean that there is no division of labor within co-operative action research. It merely stresses the importance of incorporating in the total research program the ideas, attitudes, interests and suggestions of those persons in the school-community situation who, in a very real sense, are parties to the General Education program developed for the high school (p.512).

My experience leads me to believe that a critique of academic educational research very much like Fals Borda's is also well understood by teachers and workplace educators.

Deakin's work on action research

For well over a decade now, I have had the immense good fortune to have worked on issues associated with participatory action research (we often call it 'collaborative action research') with Stephen Kemmis, Robin McTaggart and a number of their colleagues located within Deakin University's School (now Faculty) of Education at Geelong. The work has been concerned with addressing the inadequacies of conventional education research and working out ways of doing educational research which are better than conventional approaches. A major product of that work has been three influential texts on the theory and practice of action research: Wilfred Carr and Stephen Kemmis's **Becoming Critical**; **Knowing Through Action Research** (Carr and Kemmis, 1983); Stephen Kemmis and Robin McTaggart's (1988) **The Action Research Reader**: and Stephen Kemmis and Robin McTaggart's (1988) **The Action Research Planner**. These texts have been complemented by a range of other publications, reports and papers which discuss various aspects of the practice as well as the theory of action research (see, for example, Henry and Edwards, 1986; Henry, 1991; Kemmis, 1988; Kemmis, 1992; McTaggart, 1987; McTaggart 1992).

A central theme in Deakin's work has been, and continues to be, that educational improvement and reform depend on popular participation in educational research. The proposition is that there is more to educational research than others trying to understand, explain and provide ready made solutions to teachers', workplace educators' (and other educational practitioners') problems: more to reconstructing schooling and workplace education than supplying off-the-rack solutions for teachers and 'trainers' to adopt or apply.

Building on both positivist and interpretive educational research, Wilfred Carr and Stephen Kemmis (see ***Becoming Critical***), especially chapter 5) have argued that any adequate or justifiable way of conducting educational research must satisfy five formal requirements. It must

(i) reject positivist notions of rationality, objectivity, and truth, and resist, in particular, the positivist idea that all educational problems are technical problems (problems of how to achieve agreed ends) which can be solved by finding technical solutions;

(ii) accept the interpretivist argument that educational research and theory must be grounded in the self-understanding of educational practitioners, and recognise the need to employ the interpretive categories of teachers (and other participants in educational processes) in developing educational research and theory;

(iii) in addition to recognising that educational research and theory have to be grounded in the self-understanding of teachers (and other educational practitioners), also provide ways of distinguishing ideologically distorted interpretations from those that are not, as well as providing a view of how distorted self-understanding is to be overcome;

(iv) realise that many of the aims and purposes that people pursue are constrained by social structure over which they have little control and, consequently, be concerned to identify those aspects of the existing social order which frustrate the pursuit of rational goals and offer theoretical accounts which make teachers (and others) aware of how they may be eliminated or overcome;

(v) be practical in the sense that the status of educational theory is determined by the way in which it relates to practice.

Action research enters this picture as a way of moving from the theory to the practice of better educational research. As we have come to understand it, action research is a form of self-reflective enquiry undertaken by participants in social situations in order to improve the rationality, justice and effectiveness of (a) their own social practices, (b) their understanding of these practices, and (c) the institutions, and ultimately the society, in which these practices are carried out. It involves participants in planning action (on the basis of reflection on their experience); in implementing these plans in their own action; in observing systematically this process; and in evaluating their actions in the light of evidence as a basis for further planning and action and so on through a self-reflective spiral. In general terms, we would say that the common project of action research has several aspects. Every participant would undertake:

- to improve his or her own work and the way it is understood ('theorised');

- to collaborate with others engaged in the project to help them improve their work; and

- to collaborate with others in their own separate areas of endeavour to create the possibility of more broadly informing (and theorising) the common project of improvement, as well as to create the material and political conditions necessary to sustain the common project and its work.

Action research thus has an individual aspect - action researchers change themselves; and a collective aspect - action researchers work with others to achieve change and to understand what it means to change. That is, action research is concerned simultaneously with changing individuals, on the one hand, and, on the other, the culture of the groups, institutions and communities to which they belong. It is important to emphasise that these changes are not impositions: individuals and groups agree to work together to change themselves, individually and collectively, and to document the nature of, and changes in, their work.

Put simply, action research is a way in which groups of people can organise to create the conditions under which they can learn from their experience and make this experience accessible to others. That is, action research is not only about learning from experience; it is about knowledge production and the improvement of practice in socially committed groups. A distinctive feature of participatory action research is that those affected by planned changes have the primary responsibility for deciding on courses of critically informed action which seem likely to lead to improvement, and for evaluating the results of strategies tried out in practice.

In action research projects, academics and other practitioners (such as teachers or workplace educators) are joined by a common concern or commitment to inform and improve a particular practice. When people with different but complementary expertise and experience are able to work together, the possibility exists of problematising the work of both parties and of diversifying the value commitments people must attend to, justify, implement and examine. When academics and action researchers (such as teachers or workplace educators) are able to share their different but complementary expertise and experience, both stand to benefit.

In order to emphasise the kind of relationships which are essential in participatory action research, Robin McTaggart (1987) has proposed seven principles which indicate the manner in which academic researchers should work with teachers, and other people involved in educational practice. These principles represent a commitment to:

(i) teacher and community self-determination, and assisting teachers and other community members to take a leading role in reforming schools and school communities;
(ii) fostering the exploration, understanding, and practice of increasing community control of schools and curricula;
(iii) engaging teachers and other community members in research as a means of encouraging them to adopt a research stance to teaching and to educational practice more generally;
(iv) making courses for teachers and other community members practice-based, that is, deliberately enabling courses to be used by teachers and other community members as explicit means of exploring and extending their potential as teachers and contributors to educational renewal and reform;
(v) developing increasing autonomy and responsibility among teachers and other community members, and enabling teachers especially to construct their own model of teaching and curriculum by providing opportunities for self-initiated and self-directed enquiries;
(vi) emphasizing the interrelationship of theory and practice and encouraging teachers, and others where appropriate, critically to reflect on theories by reference to practice, and to reflect critically on actual practices by reference to available theories;
(vii) making the pedagogy of courses explicit and self-disclosing so that participants can reflect critically on how the activities of the course have related students, teachers, knowledge and learning context.

McDonald's, republicanism and Botham's early departure

If what has been said immediately above might be construed as a summary of some of the central commitments evident in Deakin's theory of action research, the remainder of the paper is an attempt to illustrate the practice of that theory. What follows is an example of vivencia, or shared life experiences, which is intended to convey some of the effects of our efforts to practise action research in collaboration with others, including teachers and workplace educators in Australia and Canada. My hunch is that reading participants' stories of their experience of action research is likely to be more informative about the nature of the reality of our work than my writing explicit reflections (Van Manen, 1991, p.509).

Just before I introduce the example of action research, however, might I try to explain the title of this paper and what McDonald's, republicanism and Botham's early departure have to do with Deakin's work on action research? The title of the paper is meant to highlight two obvious changes in Australian culture that have occurred over the last fifteen or twenty years, one arguably more positive than the other. One obvious change in the way of life of most Australians is the result of the presence of a range of multinational companies in the Australian economy. McDonald's hamburger chain, with its uniform buildings, look-alike personnel, standardised products, and instrumental social relations is a symbol of this change in Australian culture. A second obvious change in the way of life of most Australians over the last two decades has been a changing regard for Britain and British institutions. Contemporary expressions of republican sentiment symbolise that general change in Australian cultural values, but the difference between Australian and British perspectives on British institutions is illustrated more explicitly by an event which occurred in February 1992 at the official dinner held in Melbourne on the eve of the final of the (cricket) World Cup. The entertainment for the evening included a popular impersonation of the Queen by a well-known male comedian (with an Irish name). The comedian's act, usually well received in Australia, failed to amuse some members of the audience, most notably Ian Botham who stormed out of the dinner in protest at what he found objectionable treatment of the monarchy. Headlines in newspaper accounts of the incident the following day read, 'Botham's Early Departure'.

Notions of (i) standardisation (represented by McDonald's marketing strategy), (ii) changing relations of power and authority (represented by the Australian republican movement, and protest over attempts to undermine valued traditions and institutions (represented by Ian Botham's refusal to condone public ridicule of the monarchy) suggest criteria by which Deakin's action research work might be evaluated. A way of beginning such an evaluation would be to ask:

(i) if like McDonald's, we have contributed to cultural standardisation, uniformity and a mind-numbing compliance with our sales pitch? or (ii) if like the proponents of republicanism, we have helped to challenge the perpetuation of out-dated power relations by altering the dominant view of who knows about education and can know? or (iii) if like Ian Botham, we have stood up for action research traditions which matter, educational traditions which matter, and democratic traditions which matter?

Clearly, the work has its limitations, but if someone of the stature of Orlando Fals Borda can admit to worrying problems of work conception, failure, misunderstanding, and polemics, why should we be afraid to admit our capacity to do the same? More significantly, in our view **the work** shows what a more democratic form of educational research looks like on the ground, and indicates how such work might be practised more extensively.

It may be that we deserve to be accused of failing to realise our aspirations; even of losing sight of the golden thread that runs through all action research worth the name. If so, perhaps I should throw myself on the mercy of the court. My own inclination, however, is to obey Horace Rumpole's imperative: never plead guilty!

One example of an action research project

[There were three examples in Colin's original paper presented at the CARN Conference, 1992. Space permits only one example: Editors]

What follows is an account of an action research project written by a teacher. The names of people, places and institutions have been changed in the account.

Action research in a curriculum research project

This account of action research 'in action' is a report written by a teacher at the conclusion of her participation in a larger project sponsored by the Australian Human Rights Commission. The Human Rights Commission project was an exercise in participatory curriculum research, evaluation, and development based on teachers' exploration of a set of curriculum materials produced within the Commission

(Pettman, 1984) for use by teachers. During the short, but eventful, two year 'life' of the project (between February 1985 and December 1986), approximately 250 practising teachers, located in a wide variety of types and levels of schools in each of Australia's states and territories, participated in practical school-controlled investigations designed to enhance our understanding of ways of improving respect for, and observance of, human rights in and through schools. A major concern of the project was to practise the principles of the Human Rights Commission in its work with teachers. As a result, the project was less informed by

the image of the teacher as a replaceable operative - a counterhand reheating pre-packaged courses for general consumption ... [than by] the contrasting image of the curriculum worker as a free-standing intellectual - an arbiter of truth, virtue, and taste (Hamilton, 1986, p.22).

In slightly more detail, the project tried to embody a way of working with teachers which:

(i) regarded the curriculum materials prepared for teachers as an object of investigation, rather than a prescription teachers were expected to use as instructed;
(ii) was intended to give teachers a genuine role in planning, conducting, and reporting studies of the curriculum in use, rather than training teachers to use the curriculum in predetermined ways;
(iii) adopted the methodology of participatory action research and multi-site case study as a means of accumulating knowledge about the contribution teachers, students, and other members of schools communities might make to improving respect for, and observance of, human rights in and through schools; and
(iv) was informed by the image of teachers as critical analysts of curricula, educational practices, and educational institutions, rather than as passive consumers of curriculum products.

The following report is one of approximately 250 reports written by teachers who participated in the Human Rights Commission project.

TEACHING FOR HUMAN RIGHTS IN THE YEAR 10 RELIGIOUS EDUCATION PROGRAMME AT SAINT MARY'S COLLEGE: TERM 2, PEACE AND JUSTICE.

Carol Evans
November, 1986

a. Brief background

I have been a teacher at Saint Mary's College (Year 7-10) for the last six years. During this time I have developed a particular interest in the life options for girls from non-English-speaking backgrounds in low socio-economic areas. The School's philosophy emphasises the provision of the type of education that best suits the needs of our students. The decreased opportunities that I believe need to be recognised are those associated with: (i) being a girl, (ii) coming from a home where languages other than English are spoken, and (iii) coming from a low socio-economic background. Our work has revolved around developing a curriculum and structures that take into account these special features.

My involvement with the Human Rights Commission began three years ago when I began to document some of the procedures and practices developed to enhance life options for our students. It seemed appropriate that the teaching of human rights would be an integral part of this process. Teaching about issues such as justice and equality emerges from our Christian context and an understanding that the examination of these issues, both at a global and classroom level, would be important in any real growth of the students.

So, coming from what I considered to be a clear standpoint in terms of (i) knowing my students and their background, (ii) knowing the values of the School, and (iii) knowing why I wanted to teach human rights, I commenced, only to discover how little I knew. But more of that later!

b. Some features of the human rights programme

The basis of the programme was group research conducted by students on subjects of their own choice. Students had come to an understanding of what a 'right' is and were then asked to find out about situations where particular rights were denied. Students came up with the following questions:

1. Sexism
How sexist is employment? How sexist are household roles? How often do sexist attitudes lead to sexual harassment?

2. Disability
What's it like to be a disabled child at our school? In what practical ways does society discriminate against the disabled? How much do we know about disability in our society?

3. Apartheid
How do discriminatory structures get established? How pervasive can discrimination be? (psychological and emotional effects as well as physical) What are some facts about South Africa we didn't know?

4. Nuclear Disarmament
What is the arms race? What is Australia's position in it? What can I as an individual do about it?
(Later a Peace unit emerged as a result of this concern.)

5. Poverty
How is poverty created and perpetuated? How does it affect people's rights? What can I do about the global situation?

6. Youth Rights
What are my rights as a 16 year old? What contradictions are there in terms of society's expectations? What are the best ways of asserting my rights?

It would require too lengthy a discussion to go into everything which emerged from the six issue areas, so I would like to be selective in presenting some ways in which these questions were answered and how other questions consequently emerged.

c. Some findings of the programme
About sexism
What started off as an intellectual exploration of a reasonable stance, 'It's wrong to think of women as being inferior to men', revealed an emotional, intuitive battle that was hard to fight. It was a very assertive group of students who presented their findings on sexism in our society, and an enthusiastic teacher who applauded their work. The group had telephoned various representatives of male-dominated

areas of employment to ask if a female was employed and if not, why not. They rang the local ambulance service, fire brigade, electricians, and motor mechanics.

The findings of the group included:
(a) Many domains of work are still considered male preserves by men. (Quote from a male Ambulance Service employee: 'Oh, no, we couldn't have women here.')
(b) Perceptions of what is required to do particular jobs reveal sexist prejudices. (Quote from a member of the Fire Brigade: 'A woman couldn't do the heavy work required.')
(c) On the whole, women still don't see themselves as being suitable for many jobs in the male dominated workforce. (Quote from an electrician: 'Women just don't apply for the jobs.')
(d) The group's findings on role in their households confirmed the impact of traditional attitudes on both male and female roles (Quote: 'My mother likes to do the cooking and washing. She thinks it's her job.')

In our general class discussion some students had claimed, 'My husband and I are going to share everything'. They also recognised the need to change social structures if truly equal partnerships were to occur. However, the girls were not as enthusiastic about exploring non-traditional fields of employment, and their work experience choices later revealed as much.

The issue of sexual harassment prompted heated discussion. The majority of girls said they had encountered some form of harassment, either of a verbal or physical kind. It is necessary, at this stage, to state that before such issues can be discussed with honesty, a feeling of trust and respect needs to be developed in the classroom. I had spent much of the year trying to build that through various means.

The psychological impact of sexual innuendo should not be underestimated. The girls' outrage at being prey to verbal abuse, on the grounds of their being female, was clearly expressed. The class proclaimed in unison that we as women need to be more assertive and not feel intimidated by insulting male remarks. The intellectual stance was clear. I felt the issue had been successfully explored.

As it turned out, it had not. Intellectual viewpoints do not automatically change emotional responses. A few incidents in the classroom over the following weeks proved this to me once again.

(i) I was called in to mediate with my class and their female Science teacher over what could be considered a generally poor student/teacher relationship. The teacher had been angered and disappointed by their lack of co-operation and interest. The class recognised their actions but felt justified in behaving the way they did. The question was, 'Why?'. After a lengthy discussion, a few issues began to emerge. 'Miss X isn't firm enough with us. She lets us get away with anything.' 'Her voice isn't loud enough.' 'She can't control us; not like Mr Y.' The obvious problem of authority in the classroom was the root of their discontent. The students' perception of authority was influenced by male characteristics. Mr Y is their Physical Education teacher who uses a loud voice, can be aggressive, and uses frequent punishment. The class consequently co-operates. As a few of the girls have told Mr Y, 'It's not because we respect you, it's because we're scared of the consequences.' Miss X, the Science teacher, had not instilled enough fear in them. Was it a coincidence that one was male, the other female? Some further prompting revealed, 'We had written off Miss X the moment she walked in the classroom at the beginning of the year. I thought she was an easy-going young female teacher we could walk over.' I prodded further, 'But isn't that sexist? What were we saying about sexism being unjust?' I would like to be able to say that all the girls recognised their unfair attitude and the situation improved. However, it has not. While, intellectually, students can recognise that they should be supportive of co-operative gestures made by this teacher, they still find it difficult to respond positively unless the teacher is almost aggressive. The 'gentle' female teacher is overshadowed by the 'strong' male teacher.

There is not such a clear distinction between male and female teachers at every level of the School. Once students get to know teachers as individuals and a relationship is established, a more co-operative atmosphere is normally created. However, when students spend minimal time with teachers, their prejudices, 'easy, young, female', are not easily dispelled. The exterior characteristics of authority, loud voice, aggressive body gestures, verbal abuse, not only take over, but students allow this to happen. Knowing your prejudices and acting on them are two different things.

(ii) The second incident which supported this idea occurred a few days later as girls discussed the coming social. What would they wear? Who would they meet? What would they do if no-one asked them to dance? My natural response to the last question was, 'Why don't you ask a guy to dance?' 'Oh, no, we couldn't!' 'Why not?' 'We're girls.' They recognised again their sexist attitudes but felt unable to change. To break with tradition was too difficult.

(iii) A classroom discussion revealed the dilemma associated with becoming more aware of your rights. A student commented, 'Really, I'd love to be a housewife and look after my husband and children but I'd feel guilty knowing women should take an equal part in society.' I tried to point out that the difference between her and women of previous generations was that she had a choice; a conscious decision could be made. But she felt that once you are aware of new possibilities, you cannot cling to your old dreams in the same way.

(iv) Finally, at a teacher auction, a young female teacher was 'sold' for $2.20. Mr Y was 'sold' for $36 and bought by one of my students. She had paid a high price for his attention. No other female teacher was sold for anywhere near that price. One student commented, 'Aren't we sexist?'

About nuclear disarmament and peace
I would like next briefly to describe an incident which highlighted for me the difficulties of translating theory into practice. The issue of nuclear disarmament prompted much discussion around peace. How can we make a peaceful world? We had agreed that peace begins within oneself and within the home. Students had decided to take some positive action and try to resolve conflict in their home situations by peaceful means. Recognising that this was not easy to achieve, we decided we would monitor the situation regularly by talking in class about issues involved, such as communication skills. A distraught student approached me after class one day and confided, 'I tried to talk to my father last night about the nuclear arms race and he told me to shut up. I said we are all entitled to free speech as we are all equal. He hit me. I told him that was a stupid way of expressing himself. Violence doesn't solve anything. He hit me again. I hate him. I hate him so much.'

From this I learned a lesson I needed to learn again. The values we teach at school, even those as basic as human rights, can conflict with the values at home. Potentially explosive situations can occur. It is important to make students aware that they should not accept values that leave them powerless. If they do, pragmatism will win through and their survival will contradict their ideals.

d. Conclusions
The outcomes of this programme were many and varied and I have selected only a few to illustrate what I feel are some principles or learnings that have emerged. The incidents I have related suggest more questions than answers. They highlight, for me, the realisation that although teaching human rights is difficult and complex, it is very much worthwhile. The struggle involves examining prejudices that

are deeply entrenched, about issues where recognition alone is insufficient. It involves conflict, when peace is seen as an ultimate goal. And finally it involves empowerment, giving students not only an awareness of their rights but also an awareness of ways of asserting them that are possible and acceptable.

I realise that these are questions that we, as educators, have faced for a long time. How do you teach values? How do you get students to own values? However, it is important to keep asking these questions and to keep on attempting to reclarify the issues.

My class is certainly more aware of their rights and their personal prejudices, and the part they have to play. But it's not the end of the road. Hopefully, enough interest and awareness have been raised so that students can continue to ask questions and seek their rights. Personally, it has been an interesting and informative experience, teaching me that I still have much to learn!

References

Carr, W. and Kemmis, S., *Becoming Critical: Knowing Through Action Research* (Geelong: Deakin University Press, 1983).

Collier, J., 'United States Indian Administration as a laboratory of ethnic affairs' in Social research, 12, pp.265-305 (1945).

Corey, S., 'Action research, fundamental research and educational practices' in Teachers' College Record, Vol. 50, May, pp. 509-514 (1949). Reprinted in Kemmis, S. and McTaggart, R. (Eds.), *The Action Research Reader* (Geelong: Deakin University Press, pp. 63-65, 1988).

Elliott, J., 'What is action research in schools?' in Journal of Curriculum Studies, 10/4, pp.355-357 (1978). Reprinted in Kemmis, S. and McTaggart, R. (Eds), *The Action Research Reader* (Geelong: Deakin University Press, pp.121-133, 1988).

Fals Borda, O., 'Investigating reality in order to transform it: The Colombian Experience' in Dialectical Anthropology, IV/I, March, pp. 33-55 (1979). Reprinted in Kemmis, S. and McTaggart, R. (Eds.), *The Action Research Reader* (Geelong: Deakin University Press, pp. 291-313, 1988).

Fals Borda, O., 'The application of participatory action research in Latin America' in International Sociology, II/4, December, pp. 329-347, 1987).

Fals Borda, O., *Knowledge and People's Power: Lessons with the Peasants in Nicaragua, Mexico and Colombia* (New York: New Horizons Press, 1988).

Fals Borda, O., 'Evolution and convergences in participatory action research': a Paper presented at the Participatory Research Conference,

'A Celebration of People's Knowledge', University of Calgary, Calgary, July 12-15,1989. (Calgary: The Division of International Development, The International Centre, University of Calgary, 1989).

Fals Borda, O., 'Investigating reality in order to change it: A conversation with Orlando Fals Borda and Stephen Kemmis' (Video-recording made during the Participatory Research Conference, 'A Celebration of People's Knowledge', University of Calgary, Calgary, July 12-15, 1989.) (Calgary: The Division of International Development, The International Centre, University of Calgary, 1989).

Fals Borda, O. and Rahman Mohammed A., *Action and Knowledge* (New York: The Apex Press, 1991).

Fals Borda, O., (forthcoming) 'Contexts and consequences of participatory action research in Colombia: Some personal feelings'; Chapter in McTaggart, R. (forthcoming): *Participatory Research: Contexts and Consequences* (no other details).

Fullan, M., *What's Worth Fighting For in the Principalship?* (Melbourne: Council for Educational Leadership, 1991).

Gaventa, J., *The Powerful, the Powerless and the Experts: Knowledge in an Information Age*. Draft for chapter in Part, P., Hall, B., and Jackson T., (Eds.) *Participatory Research in America* (no other details).

Hamilton, D., 'The pedagogical juggernaut' in British Journal of Educational Studies, 35, pp.18-29 (1986).

Henry, C. and Edwards, B., 'Enduring a lot: the effects of the school system on students with non-English-speaking backgrounds'. Human Rights Commission Education Series, No. 3. (Canberra: Australian Government Printing Service, 1986).

Henry, C., 'If action research were tennis'. Chapter 9 in Zuber-Skerrit, O. (ed.) *Action Learning for Improved Performance* (Brisbane: AEBIS Publishing, 1991).

Horne, D., 'Australia: Time for a rethink': (The Age, Melbourne, p.11, Tuesday, 28th July, 1992): see also Horne, D. (ed.), *The Trouble with Economic Rationalism* (Melbourne: Scribe Publications, 1992).

Kemmis, S. and McTaggart, R. (eds.) *The Action Research Reader* (Geelong: Deakin University Press, 1988).

Kemmis, S. and McTaggart, R., *The Action Research Planner* (Geelong: Deakin University Press, 1988).

Kemmis, S., 'Critical educational research': a Paper prepared for the Critical Theory Pre-conference of the North American Adult Education Association Research Conference: University of Calgary, Calgary (May, 1988).

Kemmis, S. (1992) 'Postmodernism and educational research': a Paper prepared for the seminar 'Methodology and Epistemology in

Educational Research' sponsored by the Economic and Social Research Council: Department of Education, University of Liverpool (June 22-24, 1992).

Klafki, W., 'Decentralised curriculum development in the form of action research' in Council of Europe Information Bulletin, No.1, pp.13-22 (1975). Reprinted in Kemmis, S. and McTaggart, R. (eds.) *The Action Research Reader* (Geelong: Deakin University Press, pp.,235-244, 1988).

Manne, R., 'The cruel experiment' in The Age Extra, Melbourne, Saturday 29, August, p.3 (1992): see also Carroll, J. and Manne, R. (eds), *Shutdown: The Failure of Economic Rationalism and How to Rescue Australia* (Melbourne: Text Publishing Company, 1992).

McIntyre, A., *After Virtue: A Study in Moral Theory* (London: Duckworth, 1988).

McTaggart, R., 'Pedagogical principles for Aboriginal teacher education' in The Aboriginal Child at School, 15/4, pp.21-33 (1987).

McTaggart, R., 'Aboriginalisation involves empowerment **and** disempowerment' in The Aboriginal Child at School, 17/2, pp.37-44 (1987).

McTaggart, R., 'Reductionism and action research: Technology versus convivial forms of life': Keynote address presented at the Second World Congress on Action Learning, University of Queensland, Brisbane, July 14-17 (1992).

Pettman, R., *Teaching for Human Rights* (Melbourne: Hodja, 1984).

Pitken, H. and Shumer, M., 'On participation' in Democracy, Vol.2, pp.43-5, Fall (1982).

Rizvi, F., *Williams on Democracy and the Governance of Education* Mimeo (Geelong: Deakin University School of Education, 1989).

Shor, I., *Critical Teaching and Everyday Life* (Boston: South End Press, 1980).

Shumsky, A., 'Co-operation in action research: A rationale' in Journal of Educational Sociology, Vol. 30, December, pp. 180-185 (1956). Reprinted in Kemmis, S. and McTaggart, R. (eds.), *The Action Research Reader* (Geelong: Deakin University Press, pp.81-83, 1988).

Stenhouse, L., *An Introduction to Curriculum Research and Development* (London: Heinemann, 1975).

Tax, S., 'Action anthropology' in Gearing, F., Netting, R., and Peattie, L. (eds.), *Documentary of the FOX Project, 1948-1959: Program of Action Anthropology* (Chicago: University of Chicago, pp. 167-171, 1960). Reprinted in Kemmis, S. and McTaggart, R., (eds.) *The Action Research Reader* (Geelong: Deakin University Press, pp.85-89, 1988).

Van Manen, M., 'Reflectivity and the pedagogical moment: The normativity of pedagogical thinking and acting' in Journal of Curriculum Studies, 23/6, pp.507-536, 1991).

Williams, R., *Towards 2000* (London: Chatto and Windus, 1983).

WHAT I WOULD LIKE TO DISCUSS WITH YOU

Bridget Somekh

Colin, who can resist being drawn into a paper which begins with Rumpole of the Bailey? I was immediately persuaded by the idea of a 'golden thread' of ethical principles which runs through educational action research. Yes, yes, yes. It is a key starting point, because I believe that action research needs to be understood as a methodology and not a set of methods. We can go through procedures, collect data till it comes out of our ears, categorise and analyse with the greatest of care - but, if we do not continuously relate all that we do to a bedrock of principles, I doubt that our action research can have integrity as research.

But what is the nature of that golden thread? You claim it to be 'the presumption of collective autonomy', and immediately I ask myself what exactly that might look like. Do you intend the term as an oxymoron ('a rhetorical figure by which contradictory terms are conjoined so as to give point to the statement or expression': Standard Oxford English Dictionary)? Or are you unaware of the contradiction? In what sense can action research, in which I construct knowledge through reflecting upon data relating to my own practice, and then take action to bring about improvement in my practice, be either autonomous or collective? I might fall into the trap of believing it was autonomous, forgetting the extent to which my values and understandings are shaped by the context in which I work (through my colleagues, my students and our institutional setting), but it would be hard to reconcile this personal reflexivity with a 'collective' endeavour. In my experience there is always a conflict between my effort to gain a fresh perspective on my own values, through reflexivity, and my need to compromise those values for the sake of group harmony and purposeful action.

On the other hand, this is not a new problem you are springing on me. This is something we wrestled with in the PALM Project (Pupil Autonomy in Learning with Microcomputers, Somekh, 1991). In a very practical sense, could we say that children were learning 'autonomously' if they were working in collaborative groups round a computer? If we saw 'autonomy' according to Papert's Piagetian model of 'children as builders of their own intellectual structures', we clearly could not (Papert, 1980, p.7); but if we took Polanyi's paradox of the inter-dependence of 'personal knowledge' and 'conviviality', the notion of 'collaborative autonomy' became central to the nature of learning (Polanyi, 1958, pp.203-245). According to Polanyi, as I understand him, we willingly surrender our autonomy in order to identify with a cultural reference group: and thus, we construct personal meaning within a framework of shared experience which saves us from having to re-learn everything from scratch in each generation.

OK, so I am more in harmony with your definition of the golden thread as 'collective autonomy' than I at first thought. But I am still bothered that it underestimates the diversity of personal interests and the difficulty this causes when groups of people attempt to carry out action research inter-dependently. Your assumption that large groups 'are capable of both identifying educational values and priorities and acting together to realise those values and priorities' seems a little naive, and leads to a suspicion that people might go through the motions of this kind of endeavour, without any change taking place at a fundamental level. Might it not be better to be more realistic, and be ambitious for a higher quality of action research in partnerships or small groups?

A very similar problem arises for me as soon as you begin to write about 'democracy', so maybe, after all, there is some fundamental difference in our views. You seem to assume - as do the various writers whose work you cite - that democracy is 'a good thing'. Yet many variants of social organisation sport the hallmark of democracy without being true silver or gold. We have just lived through the end of the cold war; we have seen the spectacle of western politicians claiming that the problems of former eastern block states would be solved overnight by moving to a democratic market economy; and we have seen those peoples, instead, facing economic ruin and in some cases the outbreak of civil war. OK, so they had not become true democracies. But, on the other hand, why have the western democracies refused them the economic aid necessary to make their economies work? Doesn't that illustrate an important point? Democracy is a system which favours the majority and discounts minority interests. It is based on notions of freedom of speech and decision by majority vote: at best this can only be seen as a kind of **bureaucratised autonomy.** Democracy, as described by Pitken and Shumer, only gives autonomy to those who share the values and beliefs of the group. If individuals don't buy into the group's value system the democratic process will systematically disenfranchise them.

By this point in the paper I am wondering what has happened to the voice of participant-researchers. Why are the examples of action research consigned to the back of the paper? If action research is about 'transforming the relationship between academic researchers and other practitioners', why are practitioners' voices so far silent?

But I am soon won over when I turn to the next section, because the account of Fals Borda's theory of participatory action research is fascinating. I am reminded of conversations with the South African action researchers who came to the CARN conference, particularly Brenda XXX who was in my 'conversation' group: in countries like South Africa and Colombia it seems that all action research is a form of political action. The scale of possible operation is somehow larger: there is no democratic system to provide an aura of spurious fairness within which teachers (or other workplace participants) can carry out small scale action research with the presumption that they enjoy freedom of action.

But, hang on, I've got to the end of the section of Fals Borda and I still don't know about any action research he actually **did**! Is he a theorist, after all - working predominantly in just that tradition of 'logical sophistication' which he himself decries? Of course, you have had to quote him selectively - but then, why have you chosen to represent his work through accounts of his theories and not his practice?

I see now that the thrust of this paper is a comparison between the ideas of Fals Borda and those of the Deakin action research tradition. The mentions of other writers are brief, and, dare I say it, tokenist? Might they be better left out? The Deakin work has been very influential in my thinking, so I read on with interest. Yes, I agree with you that these three texts, ***Becoming Critical*** (Carr and Kemmis, 1983), ***The Action Research Planner*** (Kemmis and McTaggart, 1988) and ***The Action Research Reader*** (Kemmis and McTaggart, 1988) are seminal. But, unfortunately, this also means that I cannot come to this part of your paper with a neutral eye. (Sure, I admit, I came to reading your paper as a whole with in-built partiality - I already had my own ideas about the 'golden thread'). I am immediately confronted with some familiar problems which are raised for me by ***Becoming Critical***. You choose to quote the very passages which always give me trouble. You say that 'A central theme in Deakin's work has been, and continues to be that educational improvement and reform depend on popular participation in educational research'. But then you quote that stuff from Chapter 5 of ***Becoming Critical*** about 'ideologically distorted interpretations' and 'distorted self-understanding'. I have been down this road before. Who is to make the judgement as to what is or is not 'distorted'? Who will provide the 'ways of distinguishing'? Surely not academics, for this would, in Fals Borda's terms (as summarised by you), be based on 'the presumption that universities and other elite institutions are the sole source of reliable knowledge'. Your paper has served to re-kindle the anger I feel about that passage in ***Becoming Critical*** when we are told, ***'It is clear that much contemporary action research falls short of the stringent requirements that have been set for it - both in principle and in practice ... '*** (p.210) - apparently because it is ***'plagued by enthusiasts'*** (p.210) - presumably teachers and others, without sufficient specialist knowledge, who see in action research a means of meeting their practical problems, and embrace it with consequent verve. Does this mean that 'popular participation in educational research', in terms of the Deakin tradition, does not mean giving 'ordinary people' equality of status with 'academic researchers'? Is 'transforming the relationship between the two' not intended to mean that they become equals?

I am pleased to have finally reached an example of an action research project. Here is a practitioner's voice representing a report of her action research project, and you suggest that I should use it and the others in your original paper presented at the Worcester conference, to judge the quality of the Deakin tradition. I like it. I read on with enjoyment. But, here's an odd thing: I find that 'the names of people, places and institutions have been changed in each account'. What does this mean? Is Carol Evans not the author of the example? If she is, how can her account be anonymous? If not, how can you justify publishing her work without giving her credit? Assuming that she is the author, what about the credit due to her institution for taking part in this work? You wouldn't dream of publishing a paper without stating your affiliation to Deakin University, would you? I know that there is an established tradition of anonymising research accounts, but is it really applicable in the case of papers written by teacher-researchers? Are they not authors whose work should be published on equal terms with your own?

I very much enjoyed reading the action research account. I am surprised that it does not appear to have been published previously and would like to encourage Carol Evans to explore possibilities for publishing any work she undertakes in the future.

I wonder in Carol's case why the 'Human Rights Programme', which was the focus of her action research, dealt with apartheid in South Africa, but not with the subject of Aboriginal rights in Australia.

Again, I have to admit that this a question rooted in my own experience, because at the time when I lived in Australia in the 1960s I was very aware of the 'white Australia policy' governing all decisions about immigration at that time. I am fascinated by the way in which the students continually deepened their awareness of sexist attitudes in their culture, and as I read I wondered if questions about Australian attitudes to race were among those 'questions which consequently emerged'. This is only a quibble. I very much like the way that Carol accounts for the students' ambivalence as they tried to replace the sexism endemic in their culture with a consciously anti-sexist stance.

Finally, I turn back to 'McDonald's, Republicanism and Botham's Early Departure'. I do like these icons, because they make your points strike home - though not immediately, as I shall try to explain. My 'golden thread' is not the same as yours, and neither should it be. We live and work on opposite sides of the world, framed by different institutional and political settings, relating to different schools and work places. Dialogue between us is important, but there is no need for us to conceive of action research in exactly the same way.

Your three icons illustrate our cultural difference. If I am to use them as a yardstick for evaluating 'the nature of the reality of our work', as I read Carol's account, I need to empathise wholly with their meaning. Yet, I am confused. Do Australians like McDonald's? They used to like eternal 'pie and chips' in the 1960s - so have they transferred this liking to McDonald's (I am reminded of the faux pas I made in Beijing by refusing my host's suggestion that we should stop off at McDonald's for lunch). And surely it's considered a positive thing in Australia to be a Republican - isn't it? - so why does the Republican icon occupy only the mid-way position of the three - suggesting merely a transfer of allegiance from an old elite to a new? And whatever is Botham doing carrying the banner of the golden thread? Surely, to an Australian, his early departure from the banquet, and failure to 'take a joke', would be the mark of a stuck up 'pom'(?) ... I get it in the end, but initially I was confused as I read - and my confusion is significant, because it shows the cultural divide between us. It shows that you should give to my comments and questions only the attention they deserve - as the ideas of a critical friend whose biography, work traditions and national culture have imposed a different way of looking at the world.

Colin, there seem to me to be as many 'golden threads' in action research as there are countries in the world and periods of history. But they all have an affinity. I have enjoyed your paper.

Bridget.

References

Carr, W. and Kemmis, S., *Becoming Critical: Knowing Through Action Research* (Deakin University Press, Victoria, 1983).

Kemmis, S. and McTaggart, R. (eds.), *The Action Research Reader* (Deakin University Press, Victoria, 1988).

Kemmis, S. and McTaggart, R., *The Action Research Planner* (Deakin University Press, Victoria, 1988).

Papert, S., *Mindstorms: Children, Computers and Powerful Ideas* (Harvester Press, London, 1980).

Polanyi, M., *Personal Knowledge: Towards a Post-Critical Philosophy* (Routledge and Kegan Paul, London, 1958).

Somekh, B., 'Pupil Autonomy in Learning with Microcomputers: rhetoric or reality? An action research study', in Cambridge Journal of Education, Vol.21, No.1, pp.47-64 (1991).

AND IN REPLY

Colin Henry

Dear Bridget,

You were generous to write such a detailed response to this paper.

It may be that we agree on all the **important** matters: that John Mortimer deserves our gratitude for giving us Rumpole; that action research can, but should not, be reduced to a set of instrumental techniques; that the action research community should be a broad and tolerant church; that we could do with more practitioners' accounts of the problems and effects of doing action research; that it makes sense to talk about 'collective autonomy' where the phrase means groups of people managing their own affairs; that Australians need to do more to combat racism in Australia; that liberal democracies have some serious imperfections; and that the changes now taking place in Eastern Europe are often far too tragic to leave us feeling confident that they are necessarily for the better.

There is also the matter you raise of my failing to give teachers sufficient credit for their contribution to the paper. I am resolved to fix that problem in the near future.

There are, however, some points on which we disagree, and some points which invite further comment. I am going to consider a few in each category.

Points of disagreement

Points on which I find myself disagreeing with you include those which express your irritation about ***Becoming Critical***. It is difficult to see how anyone who has read ***Becoming Critical*** attentively could fail to see that it: (i) justifies teachers playing a prominent (although not exclusive) role in educational research; (ii) argues that educational improvement depends on teachers developing a meaningful understanding of the subjective and objective conditions which shape and constrain their practice (although not necessarily on their own); and (iii) recognises that teachers and academics have complementary experience which can be pooled in the interest of educational improvement (rather than privileging the perspective of either one or the other).

I also find it puzzling that you maintain a consistently negative view of the Deakin tradition of action research. Can the case-study evidence of our work with teachers and adult educators be interpreted as just further evidence of an unrelieved record of disdain for teachers, their knowledge and their practical problems? Is no more generous reading possible?

Again, there are those, including teachers and adult educators I could name, who are likely to tire of a constant demand for examples of practice and feel patronised by those who would 'protect' them from the complexities of social and educational theory. Is it wrong to argue that we need good theories (like Orlando Fals Borda's case for participatory action research) because it helps us to understand what was previously poorly understood, to increase our options for action and to arm us against our critics?

Points inviting further comment

Points which invite further comment include the observation that I have been guilty of something like dropping names in mentioning a number of key figures in the history of action research. It could look like that. It could also look as if my intention was to show that a consistent concern for nurturing people's capacity to understand and transform the oppressive conditions of their lives is a characteristic of the best-known tradition of action research and that we need to consider exemplars from the past in judging what does or does not count as authentic action research (or at least the kind of action research we would want to practise or support ourselves).

The implication that 'Carol Evans' should have been focusing on racism and ethnicism in Australia, rather than on apartheid in South Africa, is a second point which invites further comment. I can see why you would prefer that she had engaged the issues you regard as most important. However, the grounds on which you believe your judgement about what she should have been teaching is better than her own, is not self-evident. There is also the danger that in adopting this position you may be seen to be contradicting the point you made earlier where you intimated that there is something presumptuous about academics and other outsiders claiming to know more than teachers do about the complexities of their educational practice.

Another point I find problematic is your assumption that we make 'preposterous' demands on teachers by expecting them to work with others. Of course you would be right if we were as demanding and inflexible as you suggest. In fact, however, we know as well as most that there are circumstances in which teachers have no other option but to work alone. At the same time, we also realise that people often have shared concerns and that they understand that they can usually do more in conjunction with others than on their own. For those reasons, it seems sensible to continue to recommend that action researchers work co-operatively wherever possible.

Your observation that the images I had used in defining the themes of this paper were too obscure for non-Australians left me with an impression that something had slipped past you. It may have been less confusing to make the case for: (i) diversity in education and enquiry; (ii) opposing the denial of democracy in everyday life, and (iii) sticking up for worthwhile educational traditions, in a less roundabout way. I wonder if others will be as mystified by what I have written.

Finally, and perhaps more significant than anything above, you suggest we have no choice but to agree to disagree about the nature of defensible action research because we have so little in common. From where I sit, that misrepresents the problem. The issue, as I see it, is not so much that I fail to understand your position, but that I disagree with it. My inclination, therefore, is to turn down your invitation to agree that anything anyone wants to call action research **is** action research, and to continue the debate about where to draw the line. In my view, we have a responsibility to distinguish the kind of action research we want to be associated with from that which we do not, and to make it known that there is a big difference between action research that serves to domesticate and dominate, and that which serves to liberate. In this paper I have attempted (after Alasdair MacIntyre) to argue that action research has long been associated with civilised ethical standards that are to be found in the practice of action researchers in other times and other places. There may be, for example, some affinity between the kind of 'action research' carried out in certain business enterprises (Richards, 1991) or the FBI (Sonnichsen, 1988), and the kind of people like Gaby Weiner (1989) or Ken Zeichner (1991) would support. The differences in such cases, however, are sure to be more profound than the similarities. I need to be convinced that distinguishing and exposing the difference between superficially similar and profoundly different forms of action research is a trivial matter. But that is a debate for another time.

For now, stay well.
And viva critical friendship.

Colin.

P.S. When I first saw the word 'oxymoron' I was momentarily offended because I thought it was a reflection on my I.Q.. You can imagine how embarrassed I was when I looked it up in my pocket Oxford!

References:
Richards, C., 'Management development through action learning in Australia Post': Chapter 1 in Zuber-Skerritt, O. (ed.), *Action Learning for Improved Performance* (Brisbane: AEBIS Publishing, 1991).
Sonnichsen, R., 'Advocacy evaluation: A model for internal evaluation offices' in Evaluation and Program Planning, Vol.11, pp. 141-48 (1988).
Weiner, G., 'Professional self knowledge versus social justice: A critical analysis of the teacher researcher movement' in British Educational Research Journal, Vol.15, pp.41-51 (1989).
Zeichner, K., *Connecting Genuine Teacher Development to the Struggle for Social Justice:* Mimeo (University of Wisconsin, Madison, 1991).

CONVERSATION FOUR

JILL BURTON

I am Director of the Centre for Applied Linguistics in the University of South Australia and Head of TESOL Teacher Education. Starting as a classroom teacher in ESL in East Africa, I went on to teach English to adult immigrants in Australia before moving into professional development, discourse analysis and classroom research. I was inaugural editor of ***Prospect: The Journal of Australian TESOL,*** published by Macquarie University, for five years. My research and government consultancies have ranged from an analysis of dentist-patient communication for the General Dental Council in the UK to a nationally-commissioned study on professional development and support in the Australian Adult Migrant English Program and include a four-year period as evaluator of the Languages Inservice Program for Teachers (LIPT).

PETER MICKAN

I am a lecturer in TESOL in the School of Education Studies in the University of South Australia and based at the Centre for Applied Linguistics in the University of South Australia (CALUSA). I have extensive experience in teaching English and German in secondary schools, and in language teacher education. When State Manager of the languages other than English Advisory and Curriculum Team for the South Australian Education Department, I initiated and managed the Languages Inservice Program for Teachers (LIPT), in which teachers undertook action research projects. My research and publications focus on language teacher education, second language classroom research and topics related to second language acquisition, including research on second language composition.

PETER SCRIMSHAW

By way of an indirect biography, here is a list of every nth book on my bookshelves:
   Gulliver's Travels (Swift)
   Moll Flanders (Defoe)
   Wild West Movies (Newman)
   Philosophy, Politics and Society Series 2 (Laslett and Runciman)
   The County Map of Old England (Moule)

The Times Reports of the American Civil War (Brogan)
The Times History of the War, Vol. 3
The Battle of Pollocks Crossing (Carr)
Working with Groups (Klein)
Failure of a Mission (Henderson)
The Art of Writing (Stevenson)
The Duchess of Malfi (Webster)
Candide (Voltaire)
Case Studies in Decision Analysis (Moore et al)
Literature and Revolution (Trotsky)
Rationalism in Politics and Other Essays (Oakeshott)
Getting to Know Schools in a Democracy (Simons)
Developing Information Technology in Teacher Education No. 2, April 1992
Curriculum Evaluation in Schools (McCormick and James)
Language as Social Semiotic (Halliday)
Making School-Centred Inset Work (Easen)
Curriculum Research and Development in Action (Stenhouse)
Classic Myth and Legend (Moncrieff)

MANAGING ACTION RESEARCH

Jill Burton and Peter Mickan

INTRODUCTION

One of the issues which has not received sufficient attention in the literature is the place of management in action research. The focus of attention has been on the process of and approaches to action research. We believe that management is an integral part of the process. We also believe that it is necessary to develop a management view in order to embed action research more firmly in professional development programs. Without a managed context, in our experience, action research as a deliberate professional development process remains vulnerable to the vagaries of politics, funding and individuals. What, however, constitutes an appropriate managed context for action research to flourish is crucial to the discussion of managing it.

In this paper we examine management dimensions of action research conducted by language teachers, who participated in a special inservice project funded in school settings in South Australia between 1988 and 1991. Over the four-year period of the Languages Inservice Program for Teachers (LIPT) of languages other than English, we found that decision-making processes and support structures to enable teachers to carry out research projects proved crucial to the participants' success and independence as teacher-researchers.

The management of action research can be viewed from two perspectives: from the perspective of the enabling structure or management process, and from the perspective of the individual action-researcher's management of the enquiry process. The former is concerned with the establishment of conditions for conducting action research. The latter refers to the personal management required of the action researcher, who engages in the structuring of experience and enquiry to achieve certain ends. Individuals, in choosing to participate in action research, do so purposefully and, often, with some outcome in mind. The structure and order adopted through the research process at least in part constitute the management of self and context. The analytical process of enquiry also sets in train the development of a critical understanding of context as part of the process of self-management.

It is in these two senses that we believe action research and management to be inseparable. We argue, therefore, that it is important for action researchers to consider the implications for themselves both as managers of and as being managed in action research.

Management and professional development

Management is an important aspect of professional development programs in general. In a review and analysis of case studies of exemplary teacher inservice programs (Department of Employment, Education and Training, 1988) the following management concerns were identified as features of effective programs:

◆ a favourable climate for creating a learning community;
◆ the provision of active external support;
◆ effective administrative leadership.

Similarly Dunlop (1990) identified the characteristics of successful professional development activities. Amongst the eleven characteristics he categorised were:

◆ sound leadership;
◆ access to support materials and equipment;
◆ the provision of time for teachers to work together.

The above features relate directly to the management of professional development. These features, together with other factors - such as sense of ownership, application of adult learning principles and linking theory to practice (Dunlop, 1990) - create the conditions for successful professional development.

Action research and management

According to Grundy and Kemmis (1988, pp. 322) action research has two essential aims: to improve and to involve. It aims to improve in three areas:

1 the improvement of a practice;
2 the improvement (or professional development) of the understanding of the practice by its practitioners;
3 the improvement of the situation in which the practice takes place.

Action research in other words is expected to stimulate professional change in individuals. Such change and improvement may also be the goal of projects, institutions and systems. However, even when this is the case, the research processes put outcome control in the hands of researchers; and, while there is something inherently contradictory in the notion of empowering people to do research, it is nonetheless true that conducting research gives researchers the tools to critique their professional environments. This 'power' is frequently offset by system management of resources and input. A system-need to bring about professional renewal economically, or to inservice a new syllabus or set of curriculum guidelines which relies on an existing body of knowledge, may subvert professional development goals of exploratory teaching and professional self-discovery. For this to be avoided and for the control and ownership of action research to remain with practitioners, the role of management is to provide a supportive context for teachers to undertake action research on issues of importance to them.

In his reflective paper on facilitating action research in schools, Elliott (1985, pp. 259-260) set out principles for what he terms 'enabling conditions' for facilitating action research in schools. These enabling conditions match the factors identified as features of exemplary inservice practices. They highlight the critical role management has in supporting action research.

In the four-year project outlined in the next section, the project managers, although working within an organisational system, took a broad view of action research management. Their view encompassed:

Self management
- teacher evaluation and reflection on practice through action research leading to professional renewal;
- an inservice program responsive to participating teachers' levels of development and expressed professional needs.

Support structures
- the provision of teacher release time to assist the conduct of research;
- the ready availability of reading materials and individual professional support;
- an organised networking structure for peer support;
- a range of inservice delivery modes to support teachers conducting action research in different teaching environments.

Project management
The Project Co-ordinator, Peter Mickan, was supported by a project officer, project evaluator and support staff. The facilitators who ran the network groups also carried out research projects and created important links between the Project team and the teacher-researchers.

Essentially, the Project team's management aim was to provide teachers, through the Project process, with opportunities for informed choice; and the chance to make professional decisions, to reflect and critique their own and others' research and assumptions, and to share professional knowledge and skills

Project characteristics
The Project ran each year from 1988 to 1991 for primary and secondary school language teachers in the state, Catholic and private systems in South Australia. The Project and the research process, in which more than 300 teachers participated, is reported in the evaluation studies of Burton (1989, 1990, 1991 and 1992). With some annual variations, the following features were characteristic of the Project each year:

Support and training
Teachers received training in action research processes through input sessions and collaborated in network groups, which aimed to assist their research through peer support and further input, led by trained facilitators. A central databank of support resources was developed and maintained.

Research and publication
Teachers undertook an action research project connected with their language teaching during their participation in LIPT and wrote up their action research project for publication and sharing.

Research as professional development
Through participation in the Project, language teachers learned about research processes and developed reflective skills which enabled them, through further experimentation and research, to develop their teaching and curriculum skills.

Research as social action
Through the critical community formed each year, participants conducted research with others in ways which led them to project beyond the data from their own classrooms to collaborative research which could embrace wider social domains.

MANAGEMENT IN ACTION

In this paper, we present and discuss extracts from the evaluation of Year 3 of the four-year Project (Burton, 1991). In the evaluation, eleven case studies were conducted of language teachers participating in LIPT in 1990. The case studies cover the broad range represented in LIPT 3 of educational contexts and teaching locations, languages taught, and of teachers' teaching experience and training and language expertise. The data were collected from individual interviews, observations of network meetings and group consultations. The two extracts exemplify the levels and kinds of management which we found had impact on teachers' decision-making as managers of their own research and the implications of which we experienced as members of the Project management team.

The demands of action research
All participants in the LIPT Project were expected to undertake a classroom action research project extending over a ten week term. The opening extract from a Project team meeting from Year 3 illustrates the responsibility the team felt would make the Project experience manageable for participants without removing individual responsibility from teacher-researchers.

Extract 1

'We [the Project Team] have a mission to investigate and treat the problems teachers face in schools as well as to provide programs which make teachers independent and resourceful in individual times of need ... Teachers need real outcomes for their efforts, and this mode of operation [the speaker was recommending a change in the Project process which would structure teachers' participation more and reduce their responsibility for outcomes] would enable us to explore at the level of classroom operation. It would make life easier for teachers; there would still be an underlying skill development aim, but at a manageable level, one at which we could all maintain our sanity.'

'But teachers have been so positive about [doing] action research in the past that it would be hard to justify removing it [that requirement].'

'Yes, but doing action research projects within such a short space of time prevents many teachers from going below the surface of their teaching. It isn't enough in a report to write that you "feel" something is so.'

'The process of action research, rather than its content, is what LIPT is about, though. That is the in-depth part of LIPT.'

'That's too big a luxury. You need more emphasis on practice than research.'

'Maybe it's more a problem of the action research project having been built up in the minds of teachers as more important than it actually is?'

'No, it's more than that. We should be providing teachers with the tools to take into the classroom to get answers to their questions, rather than training teachers to develop their own tools [and be self-reliant]. We shouldn't be trying to transform teachers into researchers. We should help them cope on an immediate basis rather than in the long term.'

'But LIPT philosophy aims to train teachers to use knowledge, skills and resources - for that they need to develop a metalanguage.'

'Well, I think we should allow teachers to avoid terminology and conceptualisation if they find it difficult. We should have a program which allows them to stop before doing action research if they want to.'

'Yes, well, for some, I guess, the continued destablising effect of exploration is in itself frustrating.'

The Project was designed to enable teachers to determine and control their own research activity; in practice, some teachers found selecting a research topic, data gathering and documentation demanding in time and concentration. Such an open-ended process tended to trigger an unmanageable chain of action and reaction. Thus, action research proved a stressful experience - a stress which, as Extract 1 indicated, some viewed as an avoidable luxury with the demands of day-to-day teaching.

Was action research widely experienced as stressful? Evaluations, even formative ones, convey only a partial picture of the events they seek to portray: aspects, episodes, a series of timed exposures. It would be possible, unintentionally, to collect data only of teacher stress in a formative evaluation or only of teacher euphoria in a retrospective process. Our data revealed, however, that for most teachers who participated in LIPT there was a typical pattern, shown in Figure 1:

Figure 1: Participant's perceptions of manageability

TASK	RESPONSE
Understanding the aim of the LIPT project	Initial anxiety
Understanding the aim and nature of action research	Moderate anxiety which ebbed and flowed with the process of the project
Deciding upon an action research topic and process	Considerable anxiety initially*
Data collecting	No remarkable anxiety unless the process being used involved the teacher substantially in extra work.
Data analysing	No remarkable anxiety unless the process revealed totally unexpected information*
Reporting the action research	Considerable anxiety initially as most teachers have not before written for publication (i.e. for other professional colleagues to read)*
Evaluating LIPT and the usefulness of action research individually	Considerable experience of success, pleasure, and growth in personal professional confidence

*At these points, project management through the facilitators and the networks was crucial in overcoming anxiety and enabling teachers to identify rewarding amounts of stress i.e. individually manageable projects which would be personally revealing in constructive, manageable ways.

Experiencing action research

The following extract depicts what teachers typically experienced in learning to confine and manage their research.

Extract 2

E chose initially to investigate the use of computers in vocabulary development with six groups of students across two consecutive grades. He faced a common problem: how to pare down the research to a manageable level while doing something substantial, useful and interesting. Totally committed to the project, he needed to be reassured that he was considering a big enough project.

Over a period of six weeks during which he attended network meetings and received advice from colleagues and his facilitator, E conflated his research topic to investigating in one class the students' use of language in carrying out an innovative unit of work on fashion. At about the same time his desire to investigate students' use of the computer in learning vocabulary went by the board, not by design, but because the school's computer system went down at a crucial point in the data collection - a common (and, therefore, a useful) experience for would-be researchers.

At the last meeting with E as part of the evaluation, his students' study skills in the target language were discussed. Observation of the students as part of the evaluation had indicated that students were working out the task instructions for themselves and that E did not need to spend teaching time on them. The initial research question, small though it appeared, raised other classroom management questions. Crucially, E was able to admit that the reason for trying the new material was a response to a classroom discipline problem which emerged when the school withdrew use of a language textbook.

LIPT helped E to identify a teaching problem and how to deal with it. The initial stress of extra work [the research] enabled E to manage his teaching better.

The above extract reveals some of the early conflict typically experienced by teacher-researchers in LIPT between outcome demands (defining a mangeable research topic, reflecting critically on the data generated by the research, and producing an action research report on a discrete activity) and the acquisition of research and reflective skills (experiencing and developing through the process). The data of the four evaluations show, however, that most teachers needed the management requirement of having to produce a formal research outcome (the report for publication) in order to acquire the process skills which made them more independent. It was through the stress of production that teachers' goals of developing action research skills and becoming self-managing of aspects of their professional development became realistic and manageable.

Although teachers had the individual demands of conducting their own research, they also had support to draw on through the management structure of LIPT. In the next sub-section, we explore how this structure worked to support teachers' individual professional growth and renewal.

Supporting action research

LIPT teacher-researchers attended specially arranged one-day conferences during their Project involvement and they had access to a wide range of relevant reading materials and resources. They learned about action research processes and learned through carrying out research on their teaching about areas of individual professional concern.

An essential component of the support process was teachers' working together in small groups (networks) with a group leader (a facilitator). The aim of the networks was to support teachers in becoming researchers and developing reflective skills on their teaching. Though teachers worked independently on individual research projects, they had the peer support of other teachers in their network and the experienced assistance of their network facilitator. Through attending the one-day conferences for the plenary meetings, teachers also had the opportunity to network across the research community as a whole. Whereas in some (more conventional) professional development programs, teacher educators might intervene to direct activity, in this Project, teachers, facilitators and project officers worked together to form a mutually supporting, critical community.

The timing of assistance is crucial to its being perceived as support, and since people develop at different rates, support is best individualised. Group leaders, therefore, need to be sensitive to members' stages of development. In Extract 3, the importance of timing input to support the research process is acknowledged; clearly, input is found to be relevant if it matches teachers' stages of readiness or development. In the network meeting concerned, members were debating how to deal with packages of input material which were supplied to the networks during LIPT 3. In LIPTs 1 and 2, input on research processes and language learning and teaching was provided formally and almost exclusively through plenary conferences. The Project Team felt that participants could benefit from more preparation. Rather than increase the formal input sessions, the team developed study packages for use in network meetings.

Extract 3

On the whole, the network felt the action research had to take priority because of the need to get on if they were each going to finish their research projects. At this point, the content of the network packages seemed largely irrelevant. D said she hadn't even looked at the last two packages [on organising learning and learner use of language] and that she intended leaving them until later. They were very theoretical and would be worth discussing, but she was too busy now.

Network facilitators in the evaluation report are quoted as follows:

'The increased input ... meant less time for the action research. The ongoing evaluation had already highlighted the increased stress placed on both facilitators and teachers through this method.' (Burton, 1991, p. 56)

As is evident from this Extract, however, participants felt able to obstruct this intention through the self-management processes provided through working in groups and in a community.

DISCUSSION

Managing or being managed?

Theorising about teaching from research on practice has only relatively recently been accepted as part of teaching activity rather than the sole province of researchers specialising in research on teaching. Statements such as 'Enabling teachers to construct their knowledge of teaching, both with guidance and independence, is the central work of teacher education' (Freeman, 1992, p. 16) are increasingly recognised as suggesting valid ways of going about teacher education as well as validating ways of viewing knowledge. Not only do such statements recognise the social context of knowledge and the classroom, but they also legitimate the role of individual teachers in controlling and managing their professional development.

Nias (1989, pp. 155-8) argues convincingly that, historically, teaching was a solitary, relatively independent activity and that it still is. The intensity of relationship between teacher and learner, the 'box' of the classroom and, until recently, the relative freedom from the dictates of national guidelines do not encourage teachers to collaborate and build shared professional knowledge, or, even, a shared metalanguage for talking about teaching. She suggests (p.161) that it is through social interaction (for example, in groups where there are shared interests and respect) that we become conscious of our actions and beliefs and may seek to adjust or change. Thus, the deliberate creation of group structures which support teachers in critical reflection on professional practice can assist independent thinking. But, at the same time, they can create subtle pressures. Committing oneself to a greater, social group identity, even for a limited time, puts one's own identity and independence at risk - unless the group is supportive of the individual. Freeman's juxtaposition above of independence and guidance as necessary co-existing elements in teacher education programs is relevant in this regard.

It is this juxtapostion which is at the heart of our view that, for teachers to become managers of their professional environment, they need managing. We argue that carefully managed support structures in research communities such as LIPT provide both the freedom to explore and the support for development and professional growth to occur.

Leadership, collaboration and independence

The kind of leadership, and its distribution within a group or community, is a key factor in the effectiveness of such communities. Oja and Smulyan (1989) discuss two kinds of leadership in relation to the Action Research on Change in Schools (ARCS) Project. At the small-group level in this Project, leadership was shared and redistributed during the Project according to the interests and skills of group members, and changing task demands. Oja and Smulyan (op.cit., pp. 145-161) chart how this worked for one group through the different stages of the Project. Their study indicates that democratic sharing of leadership worked for individual members and for group bonding as a whole. In common with the LIPT network management, ARCS group management was premised on the promotion of professional growth and independence through peer support and collaboration.

Oja and Smulyan also discuss (op.cit., p.161) overall management of action research projects. They identify five functions:
 1 activating the process;
 2 bringing in otherwise unavailable resources and sets of knowledge;
 3 being an additional sounding-board in the reflective processes;
 4 handling the administrative aspects of the project;
 5 supporting developmental processes in individuals.

Our concern in this paper has been with the last of these functions. According to Oja and Smulyan (p.163) what is involved in this is knowing and recognising participants' stages of development, individualising the support provided, and, therefore, being appropriately responsive at the right time. We would argue, on the basis of data illustrated in the extracts in this paper, that the role of project managers is to create a climate for professional renewal - which may entail setting general targets for a research group or community but not individual agendas or schedules. We would argue, also, that a supportive climate is essential for the individual to move from increased awareness of individual professional practice to actual changes in practice and theorising about practice.

In LIPT, over the four years of its operation, although the Project Team also fulfilled the first four functions enumerated by Oja and Smulyan, most of the time - through collaborating with teachers in research activity, suggesting resources, helping teachers to clarify their plans and actions, and so on - they were concerned with the fifth. Thus, although Oja and Smulyan's second kind of management operated in LIPT, it frequently functioned in the way they identify for a group democratic process. In other words, project management can be collaborative, responsive, democratic and supportive of professional growth and independence.

Empowering leadership

There appears to be, as was suggested earlier, an inherent contradiction in talking about enabling or empowering people to conduct research or manage their own professional development. The notion of managers or professional development leaders giving power, of initiating processes on behalf of others, of providing a supportive management, suggests that responsibility remains with those who took the first step. Grundy and Kemmis (op.cit. p.334) have warned:

If action research is to avoid being 'facilitated to death', then those who preach and teach it must first of all prove their bona fides by undertaking action research into their own teaching (and their work as facilitators). And they must not only help to create the conditions under which they will become unnecessary to the practitioners whose work they will support, they must create conditions which guarantee that they will become unnecessary.

Carr and Kemmis (1986) writing on research as an emancipating activity and Cameron et al (1992) discussing the extent to which research projects can empower research subjects suggest that a research project in which teachers are both the subjects of research and the researchers can be a powerful means of individual professional growth and independence - particularly when teachers set their own research agenda, as they did in LIPT.

Certainly, the four LIPT evaluations (Burton, op.cit.) indicated that teachers found the experience of conducting research on their teaching, while supported by a critical community, a liberating professional experience:

> *'The entire exercise was,' said one LIPT respondent in the final evaluation, 'the single most valuable experience of my teaching career so far. The extended association, beyond the actual course, with other LOTE persons [language teachers] committed to being the best that they can possibly become has been an inspiration to me.'* (Burton, 1992, p.20)

THE ROLE OF MANAGEMENT

As the extracts illustrate, LIPT teachers, in facing the new experience of research, encountered stress. Without support, it is reasonable to suggest that some teachers might never have gone beyond the initial stress to the fulfilment and personal growth that most participants evidently experienced. Teachers surveyed after LIPT said that though they had planned to continue researching, they had been unable to do so without a supportive community to provide structure to their activity and input when needed.

Project management and peer support will probably always be necessary for three main reasons:

1. to support teachers who are not supported by their schools and/or educational systems;
2. to take the organisation out of teachers' hands so that they concentrate on managing and shaping their own professional development;
3. to assist teachers in establishing networks with peers.

The LIPT participants showed that even with support, action research is hard to keep going. They needed managing to manage. The support offered through the network structure brought South Australian language teachers with common goals together and they experienced, many for the first time in their professional lives, a sense of professional identity and community. We argue that management structures are essential for all such action research communities which seek to encourage independence and self-development. We believe that such structures can be creative and responsive, and, if they are themselves reflective, that they will model effectively the critical processes that teachers are working to develop.

References

Burton, J., *Languages Inservice Program for Teachers: Stage 1, 1988 - A Pilot Project (External Evaluation)*. (SA Education Department, 1989).

Burton, J., *Languages Inservice Program for Teachers: LIPT 2 Evaluation - Discussion Paper (LIPT Training Practice and the Resulting Professional Renewal)* (Adelaide: SA Education Department, 1990).

Burton, J., *LIPT: Where Next? Aims and Achievements from LIPT 1 to LIPT 3 (A Case Study Evaluation of LIPT 3 with reference to the evaluations of LIPTs 1 and 2)*. (Adelaide: SA Education Department, 1991).

Burton, J., *The Languages Inservice Program for Teachers of Language other than English, 1988-1991*. (Adelaide: SA Education Department, 1992).

Cameron, D., Frazer, E., Harvey, P., Rampton, M.B.H. and K. Richardson, *Researching Language: Issues of Power and Method* (London: Routledge, 1992).

Carr, W. and Kemmis, S., *Becoming Critical: Education, Knowledge and Action Research* (Deakin, Victoria: Deakin University Press, 1985).

Department of Employment, Education and Training (DEET), *Teachers Learning* (Canberra; Australian Government Publishing Service (AGPS), 1988).

Dunlop, R., *Professional Development. A review of Contemporary Literature* mimeo (Queensland, Australia; Department of Education, 1990).

Elliott, J., 'Facilitating action research in schools: some dilemmas', in Burgess R. (ed.), *Field Methods in the Study of Education* (London: Falmer Press, pp. 235-62, 1985).

Freeman, D., 'Language teacher education, emerging discourse, and change in classroom practice' in Flowerdew, J., Brock M., and Hsia S., *Perspectives on Second Language Teacher Education* (Hong Kong: City Polytechnic of Hong Kong: pp. 1-21, 1992).

Grundy, S. and Kemmis, S., 'Educational action research in Australia: the state of the art (an overview)', in Kemmis, S. and McTaggart, R. (eds.), *The Action Research Reader* (Deakin, Victoria: Deakin University Press, pp. 321-335, 1988).

Nias, J., 'Teaching and the self', in Holly, M.L. and McLoughlin C.S. (eds.), *Perspectives on Teacher Professional Development* (London: Falmer Press, pp. 155-171, 1989).

Nixon, J. (ed.), *A Teachers' Guide to Action Research* (London: Grant McIntyre, 1981).

Oja, S. and L. Smulyan, *Collaborative Action Research: A Developmental Approach* (London: Falmer Press, 1989).

WHAT I WOULD LIKE TO DISCUSS WITH YOU

Peter Scrimshaw

Your careful and thought-provoking paper interests me because my present job is to encourage research activities in a School of Education. Reading the paper, I wondered whether your analysis would be equally applicable to the support of our own conventional (that is, non-action research based) projects that use qualitative methods. Conversely, would comparing the management of such projects with LIPT help me to see both the management of conventional educational research and the analysis you offer of action research in a new way? These observations are a first response to these questions.

Do the problems that faced the LIPT team also face 'conventional' research teams?

Your paper identifies a number of issues and problems that faced the LIPT team; how far do the same problems confront educational researchers using qualitative methods but not involved in studying their own practice? Anselm Strauss has provided one publicly available answer (Strauss, 1987). His book illustrates how research methods are presented to students in his department as they work on their qualitative research projects. The similarities to your account are considerable. Strauss identifies the tension that exists in teams' research projects between aiming at reaching best results or furthering the creativity of team members, an echo of the LIPT team's tension between process and outcome demands. He also notes how students tend to choose too large a topic, and his descriptions of group sessions where a particular member's work or research problem is discussed have features comparable to those reported in the paper.

Strauss does not discuss overall project management at any length, but Oja and Smulyan's five functions of management for action research projects seem equally relevant to teams working on any kind of qualitative research project, while the Project team's statement of their management aims also neatly characterise what are arguably the proper developmental aims for such teams. Another similarity is that the different members of both conventional and action research teams have substantially different levels of access to relevant knowledge, opportunities and resources. While in both an enabling approach to support is possible, it is not inevitable. The set of roles too seem broadly comparable. LIPT had a co-ordinator, a project officer and evaluator, group facilitators and the teacher researchers. A large conventional project might have a senior academic as director, one or two other academics as the main (albeit part-time) organisers and research assistants and/or full time research students. Both structures are pyramidal in terms of numbers although the scale is different. In both there is some tendency towards hierarchical distribution of influence, but each has its own ways of countering this.

You distinguish between a central enabling group, the networking facilitators, and the teacher researchers as individuals. Conventional teams have these three elements too, but they are differently articulated. There the equivalent central enabling group (that is, the project director and other senior academics) is in direct contact with those doing much of the day-to-day research, namely the research assistants or research students. There is a network too, but for the conventional project this is external to the team and quite independent of it, rather than being, as in LIPT's case, an intermediate level within the total team. This network comprises the academic peer group for the relevant kind of qualitative research, and it works through the conferences, seminars, personal correspondence and journals that its members use to exchange and evaluate ideas. The balance of influence between central enablers, the network and the 'chalkface' researchers are therefore very different in the two cases.

Another difference is that the way in which projects like LIPT are usually funded means that they can provide only a temporary support structure and network for teachers. Conventional teams, by contrast, have access to a permanent national network of peers and, as part of a Department of Education, to a permanent support structure. In principle this makes it much easier to follow up or develop a project.

The two kinds of team differ also in the distribution of time between members. In projects like LIPT, the central team members may be full-time, while the teacher researchers are not. In conventional projects this situation may be more or less reversed, with the senior academic spending comparatively little time on the research, other academics devoting more to it, and the research assistants or research students being the ones who work full-time.

What this pattern of similarities and differences suggests is that the two kinds of situations are sufficiently alike to be mutually relevant, but different enough for the comparison to be informative.

What can enablers of conventional research learn from the LIPT study?

A strong theme in your paper is the relationship between pursuing research outcomes and developing a reflexive approach to research skills. This developmental aspect can be easily overlooked outside an action research context, because requests for external funding are naturally conceived and assessed in terms of what new theoretical understandings or applied practical outcomes they are likely to generate, ignoring what the proposers will learn about research methods and project management from the experience. So how in conventional settings can the professional development of research competence be institutionalised without becoming merely routine training?

The comparison also highlights the significance of the different time distributions within teams. In action research it can be hard for the project co-ordinator to get teachers to give the project sufficient priority. Maybe in conventional situations research assistants and students have an equivalent problem: how to impress continuously upon senior staff that what to the latter may be an interesting but minor part of their work is for the full-timers absolutely crucial. So what strategies do the full-timers use in each case, and are any of these transferable?

Conversely the comparison brings out the fact that in some ways, perhaps particularly in projects involving progressive focusing, the full-timer can shape the project continuously, whereas the part-time contributor cannot. So how do research students and assistants use this influence, and in what ways can senior staff or supervisors enable them to use the opportunity developmentally, rather than seeing such initiatives as threatening their own control of the work?

What light does the comparison throw on your analysis of the management requirements for action research?

Your commitment to an enabling approach to management is very important, and I share it. Furthermore, the LIPT model is clearly one very useful way of providing enabling support to teacher researchers, but comparisons with conventional research teams and their supporting structures suggests that it may not be the only one. Your long-term strategy is to see that teachers eventually take over management of their own personal research, but you envisage the support structure and its maintenance remaining the permanent responsibility of support groups based outside the schools. You also represent teacher research as very much a matter of individually defined classroom topics, where the network provides a supportive framework for helping research the topic, but not, except for practical reasons, encouraging individuals to redefine their topics. Some conventional research teams, however, define and pursue their aims collaboratively. In such teams the distinction between project directors and researchers dissolves, because both tasks are seen as the responsibility of all.

This suggests a second approach to action research projects. Perhaps teachers within a school or local community might come to view their research as a collective activity defined by mutually agreed goals, and directed at solving jointly conceptualised problems. But where then would they find the support structure to assist them? One answer, again by analogy with the conventional model, might be to build up schools and local consortia of schools as the permanent support structures that individuals or small groups need. Another requirement would be to develop a national or international network of action researchers in schools and Departments of Education that could provide additional help and advice. Indeed, CARN itself provides an example of just such an external, permanent network, independent of but supportive to the activities of specific project teams.

Perhaps too something of this more collegial perspective lies behind Grundy and Kemmis's view that those who teach action research must create conditions that guarantee that they will become unnecessary to the practitioners whose work they support. This implies to me teachers becoming full participants in the management of the support structures and networks as well as managing their own personal research. As you observe, teacher researchers gain the power to critique their professional environment. However, if all teachers have a collegial responsibility for researching their school's policies and practices too, then the scope of action research widens dramatically. Rather than only critiquing their environment (important though that is) the teachers' collective responsibility then becomes that also of changing it.

References

Strauss, A., *Qualitative Analysis for Social Scientists* (Cambridge, Cambridge University Press, 1987).

AND IN REPLY

Jill Burton and Peter Mickan

You highlight, Peter, a number of important issues in applied research, and particularly in action research, in your response to our paper. These are:

The purposes of research -
The roles of researchers -
The place of research in the researchers' professional communities.

In a recent paper (Burton and Mickan, 1993), we highlight the following purposes and reasons for classroom research:

- teachers researching their own teaching provide 'information from the front line';
- similarly, since classroom researchers are interested in learners' learning, learners can become involved as co-researchers with teachers, thereby providing more 'front line' information;
- teachers' classroom research relates directly to teachers' interests;
- teachers researching promote their own learning about classrooms;
- the knowledge teachers gain through researching their classroom influences their decision-making about teaching.

In that paper we also identify a number of constraints on teachers doing classroom research. For example, since research is not recognised as part of teaching, research does not lend itself directly to professional rewards, is not normally counted as part of professional time though it is counted as professional development, and teachers tend not to be trained as researchers as part of their pre-service training. Most important of all, in view of your third issue: teachers are not members of a research community, though they are subject to the criticisms of professional researchers.

The motivation for research by teachers and professional researchers is different. The professional researcher is engaged in pursuing knowledge in what might be termed a disinterested sense, whereas the teacher-researcher is confronting matters of significance and immediate relevance when investigating issues in his or her own classroom.

These differences may account for why teachers' classroom research, despite its success in strengthening the skills and knowledge of participants, has not become an integral part of teacher education courses in general. If, however, one accepts the importance of teachers' contributions to classroom research and the value of research as a means of professional development, then it makes sense to support teachers as researchers.

You refer to the temporary support structures in projects such as LIPT. This is also a feature of specially funded research projects in research-oriented institutions. What is lacking in all such projects are the continuing institutional features which support and promote research. Such projects are prescribed in role, function, allocation of time and research facilities.

You also note, however, another important difference: whereas full-time funding goes to managers of teacher-researchers in projects such as LIPT, it goes to the researchers in specially funded research projects in institutions funded to conduct conventional research.

One solution suggested to the concerns raised in our paper was to encourage 'collegial responsibility'. This we would argue, also. However, since for teachers, institutional structures are not in place to support them in this role, we have argued for management support of teacher-researcher communities within the school system, since where that has occurred, teachers have experienced professional renewal and have become active agents of critique and change in their school communities. Without such management or institutional support, reflections, proaction and reaction as a creative cycle of professional activity fade. Furthermore, management support actually encourages management commitment to research and reflection on practice. And finally, as Strauss (1987, p.9) points out, research 'involves the organisation of work ... including the management of physical, social and personal resources necessary for getting the research work done'.

References

Burton, J. and Mickan, P., 'Teachers' classroom research: rhetoric and reality' in Edge, J. and Richards, K. (eds.), *Teachers Develop, Teachers Research* (Heinemann, 1993).

Strauss, A., *Qualitative Analysis for Social Scientists* (Cambridge: Cambridge University Press, 1987).

CONVERSATION FIVE

MARGOT ELY

Early on, I decided that there must be something wrong with me. I adored my adopted country - but I chafed at the injustices, the promises not kept. I loved school - but it usually bored me to tears and worried me to death. I ached to be a true-blue 'American' - but I knew it was saner to be international. I wanted to be everyone's idea of a nice person - but I loved seeing things from other points of view and, at times, I took wildly unpopular stands. And so, with the true colors of a coward, I escaped into voracious reading, movies, theatre, jazz, musical comedy.

I fell into teaching the way I slip into a warm Caribbean sea. No shock! That came soon after. Never could I have imagined the intensity, joy, the fulfilment my profession held in store for me. In teaching, I could face my passions squarely, work for a humane society, help create community, learn, touch lives and be touched by them. In teaching, I could acknowledge its despicable, desperate state and still endeavor to work toward what might be. In teaching, I could learn that there was also something right with me.

JACK WHITEHEAD

I began my career in education with six years teaching science in London Comprehensive Schools. In 1973 I moved to my present position as a Lecturer in Education at the School of Education of the University where I hold a tenured contract until 2009. My research is into the nature of educational theory and my major thesis is that living educational theories are being constituted by the descriptions and explanations which individual learners are producing for their own educational development as they answer questions of the kind, 'How do I improve my practice?' and 'How do I live my values more fully in my practice?' I believe that original contributions to educational research include placing the 'I' as a living contradiction in teachers' narratives of their professional development in educative relationships with their students.

I believe that educational theory is a form of dialogue which has profound implications for the future of humanity. I contribute to local, regional, national and international networks of practitioner researchers who are critiquing existing social relations in the name of their own humanity and education.

WRITE ON: STORIES ABOUT TELLING IT

Margot Ely

Here's a quote from Elizabeth Merrick, counselor psychologist and qualitative researcher:

> *I just had a wave of 'Oh God! I haven't finished with it yet!' I need to work on it some more. How could this report not be credible? I have collected enough data to drown! I have done things 'honestly'. I have changed or hidden nothing I consider important. I have, to the best of my abilities, reported what I did and felt. If that doesn't inspire believability, what could? But I guess there is something beyond trustworthiness of the method that is important here. It has something to do with presentation. I have to ask myself: Have I made a compelling case for what I've done, what I've found? Have I made it possible for people to imagine themselves in my shoes? In the shoes of my Black, pregnant adolescents in poverty who have chosen to have their babies? In the shoes of their families, their friends? Would others be able to see, and find believable, what I've found based on what I've presented to them? I THINK this is what I am asked to consider here. HELP!*

So writes, so sighs Elizabeth.

I, Margot, receive most of my inspiration for teaching, research, and writing in what Guba and Lincoln (1989) describe as the muddy fields of qualitative research - happily slogging about with beginning and more seasoned researchers/practitioners/theorists in what has turned out to be a grand passion in my life. And so what I grapple with in this presentation has been engendered by my recent involvement in writing a book, starting the next, working as a qualitative researcher, and in teaching a course called Qualitative Field Research. This May of 1992 ended a premier run of the second half of that course. Here we focused intensely on crafting, on writing final reports. We did this by writing and writing some more and in a variety of ways. We returned to our data, added insights, collected more - and wrote. We analyzed - and wrote. We read and talked about writing - and wrote. Now, with the perfect vision of hindsight, I am amazed at my own incredible nerve for ever having taught our qualitative research course in one semester. I really had not understood at gut level the importance of writing for the entire qualitative endeavor until this spring. I'll probably learn more as I continue.

But 'writing' is too huge a process to discuss in one fell swoop.

So my aim in this paper is to push a bit further beyond trustworthiness of method up to final writing, which must surely apply, to consider with you what it might mean to write a report that is believable and interesting - a report that is worth reading. After all, no matter one's reason for doing action research, writing is involved, and almost always a final written document is part of that. The purposes for such a final report might vary - but they do exist, i.e. to help yourself make sense, gain direction, receive beginning support, receive continued support, and publish. It seems essential to me that we consider more deeply how to be increasingly believable to ourselves and to others in that document.

I want to return briefly, though, to my thought that trustworthiness 'must surely apply' to the entire research process, from its very inception on. When I planned this paper, I felt that it goes without too much saying that the shaping of a believable final product is part of a seamless whole research process - ethically conceived and carried out. But in my passion to speak of the final report, I might give the impression that it is or can be a separated event. Of course, it cannot be. Lynn Becker, a college instructor of English, says it well:

> *I think that the believability of my writing has been dependent on the trustworthiness of my method. If I hadn't done member checking or if I had been careless or dishonest in my method, then this also would have been reflected in the report. To me, the writing of final reports is a process of 'going meta' that seems to be a built-in way for researchers to check and reassess their own data. In writing it, I had to keep testing my old understandings of what I saw. For me, the best way to remain trustworthy as a writer and researcher is to find ways of distancing myself from what I have already written and concluded.*

I do what Lynn describes in my final writing. Parenthetically, I flinch some even at a separated picture of 'final writing' because I know that final writing begins the moment I put my first words to paper in my log.

There is now a rapidly expanding literature about how qualitative research may be written and assessed, I find the work of Atkinson (1990, 1992), Guba and Lincoln (1990), Van Maanen (1988), Wolcott (1990), and Zeller (1987) provocative and useful. But overall, to me, the literature on this topic seems a bit ponderous and overcomplex. Perhaps this is because writing believable research reports is also a complex matter? I'm not sure. I'll try to be plainer.

What is more, in my opinion, certainly the literature on qualitative research is far less helpful than it must be about the writing of reports. It is almost as if the authors are saying, 'Well, you've done it! You've collected data - thought about them - acted on them - and so forth. Now you're on your own with the final report. Good luck.' This is for many researchers a time of tremendous stress. I believe that in order to escape the trauma of that point, many qualitative researchers do one of two things - freeze or revert to what I call a headlong flight into more data collection. There seems to be a myth about that the more data one collects, the more chance one will have a meaningful and believable study. And I believe that this myth is promulgated by much qualitative literature.

At this point, I am ready - albeit with fearful heart - to say to people, 'Try not to burden yourself with more data than you need - with data overload. Think. Write more about your data all the way through the research process. Study and consider all through the process how your report might be crafted. Do not wait until some arbitrary point called "final analysis and writing". It is through the continuous, recursive process of thinking/collecting/writing/reading - the same process by which we create our ongoing research strategies - that our search to discover the essence of what we are studying must mesh with our search to communicate these essences in worthwhile ways.'

In this paper I'd like to highlight criteria about writing, about rhetoric of qualitative research reports because I'm of a mind that these are the heart of the matter in creating a believable and effective piece. My plan is to provide some context for what is meant by rhetorical criteria, and in this I've been much inspired by Guba and Lincoln (1989). Then I'll share the writing of some people as they plan the forms of their research reports and how this links to believability and interest. Next, I'll provide a few examples of people's presentations and their reflections on them. Last, I want to consider with you some personal ripples about the whole process.

I realize that the hallmark of many action researchers is that they study aspects of their own situations and apply some of their insights or hunches in ongoing rounds - that great continuous recursive tango. It seems important that you understand the source of some of my examples and direct quotes and how I reason that these relate to action research. While I do include the words of people who are studying themselves in their contexts - for example, Rebecca

Mlynarczyk as a college writing instructor and Judy Walenta as a nurse - most people are studying others. Their research has a dual purpose: to learn 'what is happening' with the people they are studying and to understand and give direction to how they are developing as qualitative researchers. The latter purpose seems clearly in line with action research.

In this article I use quotations from my students and graduates with their permission, and I rather freely interchange the terms action, qualitative, and ethnographic research. From this point on, there is mention of some rhetorical devices - first-person story, layering, vignettes. I hope these will become clearer as I proceed.

Rhetorical criteria talk to how the presentation is crafted by the writer so as to enlist the reader into entering the story, living it the way the researcher has experienced it, and understanding the grounds upon which the conclusions and inferences are based. The aim here is to communicate as richly, creatively, and bravely as possible the essence of the experience - to bring people to life (and this includes the researcher) - to build a story line and rhythm so compelling that there is no question but that readers choose to stay. No small tasks. But, happily, tasks many qualitative researchers find worth striving for. Usually, these rhetorical tasks are quite different from the distanced, rote ways of writing that have been our lot in the past.

Perhaps because of this history, our heads may still be back in the very transmission-oriented experiences of reading and writing that were part of our early schooling. Laurie Diefenbach, computer maven and instructor, expressed the experiences of many fledgling and not so fledgling researchers when she wrote:

> *Most of us 'learned to write' in an academic setting, but there were only certain acceptable forms one's writing could take in that setting. . . The only 'official' writing done during my school years was usually of the dead, lifeless, five-paragraph essay. ... I think many of the qualitative researchers in our support group were frightened at first because they had become so used to the 'academic' style of writing ... the cramped, uncomfortable style that is usually expected.*

In the words of Vivian Gussin Paley (1992), 'The natural connections between storytelling and learning are often obscured in school'.

Rhetorical criteria assume that the researcher produces something in writing, however raw at first. This, in itself, is not always as easy as it sounds. For Jill Schehr, school psychologist, it produced an insight about how the very act of beginning her final writing engendered her to move toward creating a believable report:

Writing always seems so definitive to me. This may be one reason why I've had such a difficult time 'writing up' my experiences. However, in response to reading Wolcott (1990) and **Circles Within Circles** *(1991), I decided that perhaps I was dawdling and creating excuses. I never do, after all, think I've gotten enough information about people ... life is so complex and reactions and feelings so diverse and fluid. I certainly did have some nascent understanding of the prison nursery community that I was part of, so why not begin to commit myself to paper? I forced myself to begin by giving myself permission this way: 'This is only an exercise. Write "freely"; this is just a rough draft.' I told myself that I was only committing myself temporarily and began to compare this writing exercise to the experience that I was having as a participant observer. In studying my prison nurseries, I observed, interviewed, analyzed, reflected ... and learned, only to find out what I didn't know. In similar ways, 'writing up' this experience enabled me to further understand and question. This, in turn, gave me more faith that I would eventually produce a credible account.*

The crafting and recrafting that are demanded by qualitative report writing highlight for all of us our concern with how language is used. Is what I am writing clear? Does it avoid the overblown? Am I inviting my readers in close, or am I setting a barrier? How do I use natural language? Does it avoid generalization? How does it give voice to the people I studied? to me? Generally, is my report reader-friendly? For some, and I am among them, these concerns with language use relate to the very core of how we wish to represent ourselves. And so we search to find a voice that is compatible with our personal vision. Rebecca Mlynarczyk, professor of writing and English, writes:

It has recently occurred to me that much of my dissertation is written in the same rather pedantic style of my male mentors - I'm thinking of people like Jerome Bruner, Howard Gardner, and John Van Maanen. Don't get me wrong. I've learned a lot from these folks. I like them. But do I want to **write** *like them? In picking up Bruner's* **Actual Minds, Possible Worlds,** *I quickly spotted the type of language I have in mind.*

She quotes Bruner as he says:

But there is a second step in literary analysis that is rarely taken. Once we have characterized a text in terms of its structure, its historical context, its linguistic form, its genre, its multiple levels of meaning and the rest, we may still wish to discover how and in what ways the text affects the reader and, indeed, what produces such effects on the reader as do occur. (p.4)

Rebecca continues:

This kind of writing does seem characteristic of a certain type of male academic writing that assumes a rather 'clear' and 'simple' stance toward the universe. Bruner's paragraph assumes that complex phenomena can be divided easily into distinct parts and can be analyzed for cause and effect. I have read so much of this kind of writing that I can easily mimic it in my own voice that emerges in my own reflective writing. ... I find more compatible the personal and probably more 'feminine' use of such devices as 'I statements' and layered stories and plan to experiment with them. I am very impressed with the power of **metaphor** *and am hoping to get away from my usual concreteness and literal-mindedness to get some of this power. There are no easy answers to complicated questions like the connection between gender and language. But I'm glad that these issues have surfaced in my consciousness. I didn't wait 47 years to write a dissertation in somebody else's voice.*

Sharon Shelton, college instructor of English, seems assured that she and others can write with cohesion and impact. Perhaps this is because she is a writer:

Hurrah to say that it counts whether a narrative sticks together, has a main point, and is effective! So much academic writing seems unclear and disorganized to me, and I view with suspicion those writings that aren't coherent and powerful. How can you trust a researcher whose narrative is muddled? If someone cannot recreate a situation, how can we trust their experience of it?

But Sharon knows that actual re-creation is not possible. After all, putting words on paper is not what happened in the classroom, on the street, in a hospital. What then is the aim for writing? For what are we striving? Rebecca grapples with this issue:

It is important to be aware of the difference between 'facts' and 'truth'. The great masterpieces of literature, works like **Hamlet**, **Middlemarch**, *or* **Anna Karenina** *are fictional, but they are also true to the psychological processes of their characters and the societies in which these characters live. Their authors have captured the essence. In contrast, works of nonfiction are sometimes factually correct but not true in the sense of getting at the essence.*

Rebecca continues:

I certainly don't wish to suggest that ethnographers are budding fiction writers, that they can blithely ignore the facts in trying to get at the truth. Far from it! The ethnographer's job is to get at the essence of what is being studied through the most accurate observation and analysis possible. Facts should never be ignored, but they are just the beginning. Making meaning of the facts is the hard part.

I, Margot, like the distinction Rebecca makes between facts and truth, and I have found the search for 'essence' to be a goal many qualitative researchers seem to understand tacitly. Tyler (1987) uses a different term, that of 'evocation' to highlight this aim. Atkinson (1992) talks of writing for 'readability' and 'representation'. He says, 'The ethnographer is undoubtedly an artisan who *crafts* narratives and representations'. But it is an illicit sleight of hand to refer to these products as 'fictions' just because they are 'made'. And the historical writer David McCullough (1992) provides what I think is a splendid thought. In describing his aim for writing, he quotes the French artist Delacroix, who said, 'What I demand is accuracy for the sake of the imagination' (The New York Times, August 12, 1992).

The idea here seems to be similar. We are striving to present the heart of the matter as we have distilled it from our experiences, knowing all the while that creating exact copies is impossible, even if we wished to do so.

And now, in a linear fashion that is never true of the recursive process of crafting an action research report, comes the question of form. What ways, devices, will I use to communicate the essence of the experience? What forms will best do justice to the people who were my participants? What data will I include so that my readers have sufficient bases to understand how I came to my insights and/or to help them come to their own? How do I create a partnership with my readers? How do I keep the thinking open rather than neatly closing it off? From whose point of view will I present the narrative - or better, how many points of view will communicate sufficiently the complexity of what I studied and learned? How can I come across as a person and as a person who is a researcher?

Jill Schehr, who previously shared her thoughts on getting started, writes now about a point in time somewhat further along:

Tentatively, I have, somewhat grandiosely, decided to produce on an epic scale. The cinematic techniques I have employed in the field reflect my wish to describe the social culture of the prison nursery I am studying. Broad descriptive writing, from an observer's view, is how I intend to present this wide-angle camera 'pan'. I have tried it, and it seems just the brush I need to paint the backdrop. But I have also learned the value of 'layering' from another vantage point. For example, while describing the social context of the prison nursery, I can 'zoom' in on the individuals who comprise this community: inmate mothers and their babies. Closer still, I can write about a mother's experience, at times from her viewpoint, using knowledge gained from hours of observation and interview. Thus, what started out to be a distanced descriptive account now comes more to life with the use of these new writing techniques.

As I became more familiar with my data, I also became more comfortable painting more 'close-up' vignettes. Thus, I painted backdrops and zoomed in on vignettes ... to my surprise, what evolved seemed 'alive' and true to my experience. I became proud of my ability to lift the 'doctoralese' censorship that had often encumbered my writing. This writing was much more personal than even I had been used to ... and why not? This participant-observer experience had touched me way down deep. However, I still have a nagging feeling that my hard work will not be taken seriously. ... I am afraid that perhaps it is too passionately painted.

In the following excerpt, Ken Aigen, professor of music therapy, shares his thinking about form. It is clear that Ken wants both to do justice to his participants and to move beyond the usual forms of discourse of his profession:

Besides having a concern for the welfare of the study participants, my respect for them has led me to want to find a way for their voices to speak in whatever form my final report takes. How a Music Therapy group is experienced by the participants is not something that has been written about extensively, but it is something which is of ethical concern and professional interest. Yet this task is quite difficult in the group under discussion because these children have significant communication disorders. One way I have discovered to get around this difficulty is to employ narrative devices such as constructs, critical incidents, and themes.

First, in order to differentiate my research efforts from clinical documentation, I thought that it would be interesting to present the therapy group as a social system, including, of course, the therapists. In this way, I would move to a level of description and analysis not typically aspired to by clinicians themselves. I also became interested in

> *communicating the evolution of the repertoire of the group, because I saw the unfolding of group process in the themes underlying the various song activities. Currently, my orientation point has been looking at the ways in which spontaneity and improvisation characteristic of therapy are manifest in the group setting. However, I am still not absolutely certain that this will be the central theme around which I organize my report of findings. In fact, it may turn out that the final focus will emerge as I put the findings into some form to be shared with others.*

Carol di Tosti, teacher and school administrator, did a study of a small number of 'Whistleblowers' on corruption in education. Here she is talking about one superintendent of schools. She calls him 'my superintendent'. He went so far as to wear a wire at meetings to record for authorities what was happening:

> *During the interviews, reading through transcripts, viewing the commission reports, I found the experiences of my superintendent to be fascinating, mythic, compelling, and topical not only for our time, but for all time. My superintendent feels very strongly about the failure of American public school education to overturn what he deems to be the murdering of children every day in our schools. He is an impassioned man. His work has been impassioned. He has, as I discovered both in interviews and through other accounts, devoted his life to serving children. His experiences of thwarting corruption in his district testify to the magnitude of his desire to thwart a system that he now believes refuses to reform itself toward producing quality life and learning. Hampered, encouraged, stirred, and burdened with my insights, I considered: Here is drama; here is a life of impact. Do I use forms which capture this life to make it vivid, vibrant, real? Or do I do what my various teachers have 'taught me so well?' 'Just do it and get it over with?' I made my decision; I had to be just to my superintendent. I had to be just and ethical to myself. I was compelled by conscience, thank God, compelled by myself, by the words of my professor and my support group to select the forms, the genres of revelation. Thus, I wrote stories, poems, acts of a longer play. As I began, I became more involved in the understanding that not only must I strive for accuracy of content (the spirit and flavor of my superintendent's drama), I must be ever vigilant about how I unfolded those dramas. To him, his life and actions held real meaning. The genres I selected should also signify and relate this meaning; the fusion of form and content should be complete.*

It is probably clear by now that in my, Margot's, qualitative research work, I lean toward writing a report in a variety of forms. There are differing opinions about that. Sticking to one form has worked well for many researchers. For example, Oscar Lewis's books in firsthand accounts have the compelling nature of fine novels to me. I am of the mind, however, that combinations of rhetorical devices function in the service of the report in specific ways. The combinations may consist of, for example, vignettes, constructs, themes, first-person accounts, layered stories, plays, poetry, 'autobiography', biographical data, allegories, diaries, parodies, songs, picture strips and their narratives, direct quotes, multivoice accounts, collage (Atkinson [1992] talks of bricolage and pastiche), and, of course, the researchers' own stories, musings, and, very important, the connecting narrative. The devices depend heavily on figures of speech - metaphor, synecdoche - that serve as tools for understanding, thinking, and feeling about the study. For me, such narrative combinations present a more fair feel of the complexities we study, better help communicate multiple realities, and more easily draw the readers in near, as well as provide distance when distance is desirable. What is more, different rhetorical forms can signal that different jobs are asked of the reader. I am not alone in this, of course. Many qualitative researchers have come to conclude that the sole use of prescribed narrative devices or those that have worked well up to now is to reduce what we can relate and closes off the possibility that our readers can create their own alternative insights. What I am suggesting is the judicious presentation of old as well as new narrative devices in the service of the report. This view of presentation counters the myth that there is 'one correct way' to write qualitative research reports.

Generalizations about forms don't hold. So, while I do not hesitate to communicate my opinion about multiple forms, I also watch carefully not to force it. In the final analysis, decisions about form must be based on what seems to the researcher-writer to be most honorable in telling the story. Thus, it is a decision about quality, not quantity of form.

In order to bring this presentation more to life, it seems fitting to share several rhetorical devices created by researchers. I offer them with the proviso that you understand they are lifted out of context; they are not the entire research report.

Lynn Becker studied life in one kindergarten. Here, as some small context for her 'Playlet in Two Voices', a section of which follows, are two of her field log entries:

On October 11th, she wrote:

I decide to spend the next few minutes at the table where Walter has been playing with the dominoes. When I return to that table, Walter is sitting next to another boy, and they are both working on puzzles. Walter is telling the other boy (William) that he will be his friend and that William won't have to worry about not having any friends in the classroom. As Walter is saying this, William silently works on his puzzle. Sue, the teacher, comes over and separates the boys to different tables.

On November 8th, she wrote:

At one point, she [Sue] tells Walter, who is sitting on a chair, that he didn't put his jacket away properly and that he should go back and fix it. Walter says, 'Oh, yeah. That's right,' and rushes back to his cubby to pick up his jacket. As he starts to walk back to his chair, he says, 'May I?' and Sue cuts him off and says, 'No, you may not get a mat. Now sit down quietly.' Walter has a pained expression on his face, and he looks as if he is about to cry. He sits down at the table and says, 'I want to lie down for my nap.'

And now, a piece of Lynn's 'Playlet in Two Voices - Kindergarten':

A PLAYLET IN TWO VOICES
Kindergarten

[Walter's voice is inferred by the researcher, Lynn Becker]

Walter: It's nap time, and I'm so glad Miss Harris let me have a mat today. Last week I was so tired, and all I wanted to do was lie down and rest before snack time.

Teacher: I'm going to put on a record that I know all of you will really like. It's from Peter Pan.

Walter: My favorite Peter Pan song. I can fly! I love this song. I have to sit up to hear this. I want so much to sing along with this.

Teacher: Close your eyes and listen carefully. Relax every part of your bodies.

Walter: I want so much to sing along with this. I have to sit up.

Teacher: Keep your body still. Relax your toes, and your feet, and your legs.

Walter:	I can fly! I can fly!
Teacher:	Keep still now.
Walter:	I'm Superman!
Teacher:	Your mouths shouldn't be moving.
Walter:	I have to take my sweater off. I'm so warm now.
Teacher:	Relax your stomachs and your arms.
Walter:	I'll just hold it in my lap and she won't care.
Teacher:	You should be wearing that.
Walter:	I wish I could really fly like Superman.
Teacher:	Keep your bodies still and lie down while you listen to the music.
Walter:	I can't sit still any more. I want to fly out of this room.
Teacher:	Put it on now. You just got over being sick.
Walter:	Maybe I could turn my sweater into a great cape.
Teacher:	*Now*, Walter!

Lynn wrote the following reflections on the Playlet:

> *I saw this particular piece of writing as more than an attempt to express classroom life from Walter's point of view. It was my attempt to understand how Walter thinks and to experience something of his struggle for a sense of power and voice in this environment. For me, this kind of writing is not 'frills' in qualitative research. It seems to be an important and necessary part. 'Becoming the other' or using the first-person 'I' helps me to get beyond the limits of being in the 'researcher' mode. This kind of writing seems to be more honest in some ways than writing that aims to be 'objective'.*

Sharon Shelton crafted several stories and poems as part of her report about experiences in a third-grade classroom. Here is a piece of Sharon's first-person story about Amanda, a third grader. This story might be considered a contextual ground for the poem that follows it. The classroom is labelled 'whole language' and is the showpiece of the school district.

NO A FOR AMANDA

Mm. Popcorn! I am so hungry. It's almost lunchtime, and I only had a bao, a Chinese bun, for breakfast. I can smell that popcorn. I want to eat it right now. But first we have to make our names and glue popcorn on them. Or make popcorn people. I know! I'll do both. Ms. Thompson will be so happy when she sees I'm doing both.

I wish my hair were blonde instead of straight and black. I'm glad my pencils are sharp. I'll draw my letters as carefully as I can. I am going very slowly on the sides of my A to make them touch each other at the top. A for Amanda. I don't want my lines to wobble. Ms. Thompson doesn't like wobbly lines.

Mimi is saying she's writing her name. I'll bet she doesn't draw a picture, too, though. I like Mimi's shoes. They look like grown-ups' shoes. I wish I had clothes like Mimi, but my mother always says we wear the same clothes as long as we can. She always says, "Three years new, three years old, three years patched."

Ms. Thompson is stopping at our desk! She is dressed in a purple top and pink pants. Pink is my favorite color in the whole wide world. Ms. Thompson looks so pretty today. She's picking up my picture! What's happening, though? She's turning it over. Why is she turning it over? She's walking away. What is she saying? What does she mean, 'Start over. Too small?' Doesn't she see my neat lines? Doesn't she know I am going to draw a girl, too?

Don't cry. I mustn't cry. Good girls don't cry in class. Start over. Just start over. Remember to make my A bigger. Remember to make my lines straight. Remember to be quiet. Always remember to be quiet.

Here is Sharon's poem that follows 'No A for Amanda':

AMANDA 1992

It feels like 1949
To me
Watching you there,
Bright sparrow eyes
Your wings folded,
Cold,
No singing.

> You pick at crumbs
> of learning
> Flung unthinking,
> Unseeing.
> Your mind flitting
> Through
> Other people's stories,
> Other people's songs.
>
> I was once a fledgling,
> Caged in silence,
> Frozen by obligation,
> Hungering for spring,
> Longing to take wing,
> Crying, dying to sing.

Sharon wrote:

> *I was happy with the poem I wrote about Amanda, comparing her to a bird who could not yet sing or fly. I identified with Amanda, and expressed great hope for her through my poem. I feel that it was coherent and had unity and clarity. I think that the poem captures the essence of the story, but I am pretty sure that the order and combination - story followed by poem - are crucial at getting at the meaning of Amanda's experience. Neither my story nor the poem alone would do that for me.*

I believe it is also important to mention here that not all classroom research pieces have been as sad as the two I shared. Indeed, in her large report, Sharon did an interesting and necessary job: she presented a sympathetic story from the point of view of this teacher, a story that highlighted the constraints under which she felt she worked. Also, of course, many people document victories ... in process and grand. The bottom line is that qualitative research holds an enlarging mirror up to our imperfections, our humanity, and I believe this is particularly true for action research. To accept this and to go on to do something about it ... only to reach another stage of imperfection ... seems the key for me. What is sure is that studying oneself usually (dare I say always?), carries with it some discomfort as well as heightened self-awareness. For example, Rebecca writes:

> *And yet I continue to struggle with my desire for control. Now, in the spring of 1992, as I transcribe the last audiotape, I hear my own voice*

far more than anyone else's. When I begin to worry about whether the students will pass the Writing Assignment Test, I 'control' my own panic by trying to do everything I can to help them although I know deep down that they need to learn to help themselves.

As the vignettes from my life as a teacher reveal, some themes have remained relatively constant: an interest in and respect for the students as individuals and as writers, a fascination with the processes involved in teaching and learning, a tendency to reflect on my practices and to attempt to change. But also running through these vignettes, almost like a litany, is my struggle with the issue of control. There seems to be an ongoing conflict between my desire to maintain control as a teacher and my understanding that, in the final analysis, only the students can control their learning.

Judy Walenta, a nurse, did her research about Sonny, a young adult labelled autistic. In her four-person layered story of one event, Judy approached what might be called a Rashomon-like rhetorical presentation. She reflects on the experience:

The pieces which I wrote in 'One Day in the Park' are impressionist in nature. My pieces are 'impressions' of a scene or, in the case of Sonny's story, a life seen through someone else's eyes, with the purpose of inviting the reader into another reality. The hope is that the reader will make her/his own observations about the scene and individual being presented and draw his/her own conclusions. I choose to present my layered story through the eyes of four people in order to help me get a better look at what might have happened on that day.

The story concerned an event that took place when Sonny was in the park with some counselors and some other residents from his group home. I had concluded earlier that he had had a seizure from the way the counselors told the story, [but] Sonny's mother disagreed and felt that the counselors were just covering up for negligent acts on their part. Sonny's story - the construct - seemed important to present. He is the silent one who speaks for himself rarely and then in one- or two-word messages. I needed to see it from Sonny's point of view, from his mom's, and from the perspective of two counselors - one who saw the event and one who was with him afterwards. I did not write the story to entertain, but as an exercise in experiencing someone else's point of view.

Michelle Haddad studied a principal on the job. Following are some pieces from what I call a construct - her introductory picture of Marty, the principal. Much of what she concludes are Marty's own words, edited and written around to present a whole 'photograph':

'I'M NOT A REBEL, JUST A MAVERICK'

It's been said that I don't care about the outside educational bureaucracy. That's not so. I don't consider people outside the school the enemy; they're just secondary. They are not bad people trying to destroy us. It's not a fight; it's just that, you know, it's what they think they need. They think they need something, and it's important to them. And the answer is, it's not important to me, or it has secondary importance to me.

Listen, I do what is my priority, which is the internal. I recognize responsibility for external authority as well because you can't just say, 'I'm not going to do anything they want or need.' They have their needs, too, and they have their purposes, but it's basically unimportant. And, of course, the other part of the responsibility that I have is I can't punish my children or my teachers by not doing what the outside authorities say they need to do in order to go on to high school. We do what the children need, and everyone else be damned. There are rules and regulations for everything, and those rules and regulations are sort of parameters. You try to the extent possible, and where it makes sense, to stay within them. But I break rules and regulations continuously.

I don't mean to say I'm always right, or that the system is always wrong, but sometimes the system makes mistakes. Take, for example, the Iraq war. We were mandated to have shelter drills. Now, we haven't had shelter drills since World War II. They said you should have the children duck under the desks. And I said no, because the kids are scared as it is that some of these Scuds might be here. They don't understand a distance of 8,000 miles away. This is wrong. They said, 'Oh, no, no, you've got to have it.' The answer was, I never had the drills. I got back a note saying, 'You have to have shelter drills.' I just didn't respond to it. I just ignored it, that's all.

Most principals did it, though. You know, it's easier not to disobey. It's easier just to do it. The answer is, you pick your battles. Let me put it this way: I'm not butting up against them as a whole. I'm really going around the side. I'm flanking them. Because, if you butt them, then they're going to fight you back. And then they have the authority to say, 'You're not meeting your mandated needs,' or whatever it is. So, I don't butt against them head-on. I say, 'Okay, I understand. Okay, I'll see you next year.' Yeah, I love beating the system, because the system stinks. It really does. And one other thing. It's lovely to have tenure.

Shelly reflects about this sort of form:

Writing about Marty in first person was and still is very difficult. I had a lot of trouble with even daring to attempt to write in first person, believing that to make a statement in Marty's voice would be presumptuous. What right did I have to assume that I could speak for Marty? My study group convinced me to take the plunge. If felt like I was holding my breath and saying to myself: One, two, three, jump! On an intellectual level, I thoroughly agree that everything is subjective, relative to interpretation, and that writing in first person is no more presumptuous than writing in third person. But it still is hard. There must be something in our conditioning as academic writers that triggers a 'dare not tread' feeling about writing that is not impersonal.

Next is an example of what I label 'a snapshot'. This one is a brief, first-person, historical picture written by Elizabeth Merrick about Marisol, a Black unwed teenager in a culture of poverty, who is pregnant and who chooses to have her baby:

MARISOL

You want to hear about my life? Well, I wasn't raised by my mom - my real mom. When I was little, I lived with my grandmother's friend. They took me in when I was young ... real young ... when I was born. My mother didn't want me. My grandmother couldn't take care of me because she was taking care of my other cousins, so my grandmother's friend took care of me. Understand?

I lived with them from then until I was about four and my mother came back to town. Who knows where she'd been. I always remember that day she came and got me. You gotta understand I was just four years old. The people I was living with never told me that they weren't my mother and father so I always thought they were and their sons were my brothers. They never told me for fear it would hurt me.

And when she came and got me, I was crying. I always remember that day because it was hard. This lady coming in and she was like 'I'm your mother' and all this foolishness. And I was screaming, 'NO! No, you're not!'

So she took me from then on until I was like seven. And she used to lock me in the house by myself. I had to wash my own clothes and cook my own food and stuff. When I got to be like 10 or 11, I knew how to ride the trains by myself and so I ran away from my mother and went back to the people who raised me.

Some narrative devices are very brief and very powerful. A colleague recently spoke of a study she came across - ***Worlds of Pain*** - in which Lillian Rubin, sociologist, psychologist, and activist, explores the experience of blue-collar families. My colleague found that she could not put it down, even though, as she read, she almost did not want to know that much. Rubin culled statements from her many hours of interviews with each family. After each statement, she identified the speakers:

> Woman, aged 28, eleven years married, 4 children
> Man, aged 32, twelve years married, 3 children

By this simple device, she kept the quoted words bound to the worlds from which they came, and she hammered home to me how young these couples were and how soon burdened. And I am reminded once again that I learn the most about writing qualitative research reports by reading the great ehnographers - Wolcott, Mead, Steedman, Paley, Spradley, Benedict.

In discussing writing with you, in particular the writing of narrative, I feel I am in danger of carrying coals to Newcastle. I am, after all, sending my messages to people who know a tremendous lot about writing - who do much writing. I am, after all, in the land of Jimmy Britten, Margaret Meek, Harold Rosen, Paul Atkinson, Martin Hammersley, William Shakespeare. But, I do feel I must make a statement now - after the fact - about how I see writing.

It is through story - through narrative of all sorts - that we understand ourselves and our worlds. Barbara Hardy has said that narrative is:

> *... a primary act of the mind. [There is an] inner and outer story-telling that plays a major role in our sleeping and waking lives ... for we dream in narrative, daydream in narrative, remember, anticipate, hope, despair, believe, doubt, plan, revise, criticize, construct, gossip, learn, hate, and love by narrative. In order really to live, we make up stories about ourselves and others, about the personal as well as the social past and future. (Meed,* **The Cool Web,** *p.12)*

My narrative represents who I am - what and who I value - what and who I disdain. It helps me to set events into time and context and links me to others. My writing allows me to consider and reconsider my actions. It is never neutral, even when I try to make it look that way. It is selective. I cannot 'get' or write everything. My writing always sends personal, political, and/or ethical messages even if I am not consciously aware of them. Because of this, what and how I write become crucial to me as a qualitative researcher and must be attended to. Awesome!

But we are in a wonderful position because of the match between certain basic assumptions that power both action research and the interactive theory of language - in this case, interactive theory about reading, writing, and literature. It is not strange to either field to believe that what we know we construct contextually, that it is partial, multifaceted, and shifting. We celebrate our subjectivity because that is all there is; yet we care deeply to link with others, to read for binding, in-process understandings. As writers of qualitative research reports, this makes it imperative to share our stances and processes in responsible ways. After all, for our readers, what we write **is** the 'field' that we have studied. The 'better' we write, the 'better' we may help people to understand and assess those pieces we saw as important. There is no escape. Our readers will not read our minds, even if we are our own readers. They will read our texts, our writing. This alone demands that we face head on some of our own ways of seeing the world.

Jill does what I believe to be a splendid job in writing about just some of the issues she found she needed to face in order to produce a credible report:

Apart from my professional experience, there are personal experiences which may often serve to distort my perceptions. I am a mother who is raising two children. In some ways, this humbling experience has made me more sensitive to the complexities of the job of mothering, and counteracts my tendency as a clinician to be unsympathetic to parents (especially when encountering abuse and neglect). But, as a mother, I have slowly developed a personal philosophy of parenting and constantly have to guard against its intrusion into my observing and writing about other mothers.

The majority of the mothers in the nursery, and general prison population, are women of color. Poverty and deprivation are often the common melody running through their stories. I have been raised in a different cultural environment. I am now immersed in a social culture with rules and customs that are diverse and, at times, very new to me. It is a challenge for me to try to 'understand' in so foreign a culture, and yet there are many commonalities that we share as women and mothers. As a psychologist, I have to consider how these different cultural aspects influence what I observe ... guarding against relying on theory for understanding. As a mother, I have to guard against judging the quality of other mothering which I may not understand as it stems from different cultural practice.

Finally, I am working with women who are behind bars. Some of the women speak openly about their crimes, while others profess their innocence. Although they have been judged and stripped of their freedom, they have been allowed to raise their babies for one year. As a mother, I have strong emotional reactions to each inmate mother who is forced to send her baby away. As a citizen, I have a response to antisocial behavior. As a woman, I am aware of the victimization some women, especially from minority groups, experience in their relationships and in their treatment by authority. It is my job to listen to their stories, remaining aware of how my biases may interfere with a new way of understanding and writing about what I observe and experience. I have confidence that my personal and professional philosophy of looking within and without at the same time will keep me 'on my feet'. It is in this area of transition between self and other that my stance as a researcher continues to evolve.

Witherell and Noddings (1991) point to the power of story - of rhetoric - to engage us in more than getting the facts when they say that 'story fabric offers us images, myths, and metaphors that are **morally resonant** and contribute both to our knowing and **our** being known.' Witherell and Noddings bring me full circle. The process of writing - of striving to meet rhetorical criteria in a qualitative research report - often has personal consequences equal to or more important than producing the report itself. I have shared with you Sharon's coming to an expanded and less negatively stereotyped picture of the teachers she studied, Rebecca's conscious struggle to understand and harness her own control as a teacher, and Carole's fight to conquer her fear to take writing risks (she calls it cowardice; I do not). There are so many other vignettes about the personal consequences, the ripples from writing, but I would like to bring only one more to your attention. Here, Judy grapples with what she calls the 'White Knight Syndrome'. See also how she uses metaphors:

With my helper/healer background, I think the greatest danger to my detachment was the temptation to cast myself in the role of savior for Sonny, or even for all of the residents in the group home. I received the most assistance in my attempts to avoid this approach by some of the participants themselves! I was surrounded by images of saviors: parents, direct care workers, group home administrators, even teachers. Several of these individuals saw themselves as the only one or ones who truly understood Sonny and other people labelled autistic. Staff defended the residents against parents, parents against staff. Administrators blamed the parents and even the school for everything that went wrong.

The only group that appeared to attempt some neutrality was the teachers, although I did not have sufficient contact with them to verify this perception.

Through all of this, I constantly worked on seeing and writing about a variety of points of view. Frequently, when I felt myself getting up on my high white charger and grabbing a lance, I consciously slowed down to a trot and initiated a mental dialogue with all parties concerned. This did not come naturally and easily at first and still requires constant effort. But it has been very rewarding. I am now much quicker to realize the white knight syndrome and to remedy it. All that armor is just too heavy, too confining.

When all is said and done, to me the greatest value of working toward a believable and effective report lies in its affirmation of the self - the researcher - as a central, powerful, flexible, fallible, learning human being. Judy puts it this way:

I know I have not captured the whole person in any of my characters; however, my own personal barometer indicates that I have represented important pieces, and, in the end, our personal barometers are really all we have to go on. More important than member checks are gut checks. Our own awareness of ourselves and what we bring to our observations and how that relates to our sense of the person or situation is what need to be constantly cultivated. To me the message is: Perceive, empathize, incorporate, change, synthesize, self-disclose, examine your own perspectives, but never, never let go of them for the sake of anything or anyone unless it makes sense to you. Your perspectives make you who you are.

Finally, as what I consider a particularly apt capstone to this paper, I offer you a quotation by Salman Rushdie (1991) - a statement about the importance of self, the importance of self in writing:

'Our lives teach us who we are.' I have learned the hard way that when you permit anyone else's description of reality to supplant your own - and such descriptions have been raining down on me, from security advisors, governments, journalists, Archbishops, friends, enemies, mullahs - then you might as well be dead. Obviously, a rigid, blinkered, absolutist world view is the easiest to keep hold of, whereas the fluid, uncertain, metamorphic picture I've always carried about is rather more vulnerable. Yet I must cling with all my might to my own soul; must hold on to its mischievous, iconoclastic, out-of-step clown-instincts, no matter how great the storm. And if that plunges me into contradiction

and paradox, so be it; I've lived in that messy ocean all my life. I've fished in it for my art. ... It is the sea by which I was born, and which I carry within me wherever I go.

References

Atkinson, P., *Understanding Ethnographic Text* (Newbury Park, CA: Sage, 1992).

Ely, M., Anzul, M., Friedman, T., Garner, D., & McCormack, A., *Doing Qualitative Research: Circles Within Circles* (London and New York, Falmer, 1991).

Guba, E., & Lincoln, Y., *Fourth Generation Evaluation* (Newbury Park, CA: Sage, 1989).

Hardy, B., 'Narrative as a primary act of the mind', in Meek, M., Warlow, A. and Barton, G., (eds.) *The Cool Web: Patterns of Children's Reading* (New York: Atheneum, 1978).

Lincoln, Y. & Guba, E., 'Judging the quality of case study reports' in International Journal of Qualitative Studies in Education, 0951-8398/90 (1990).

McCullough, D., The New York Times (August, 1992). Paley, V.G., 'You can't say you can't play: Free choice, friendship, and fairness among young children.' Address delivered at the Eleventh International Human Science Research Conference. Rochester, MI: Oakland University (1992).

Rushdie, S., The New York Times, p.88 (December, 1991).

Tyler, S.A., *The Unspeakable: Discourse, Dialogue, and Rhetoric in the Postmodern World* (Madison, WI: University of Wisconsin Press, 1987).

Van Maanen, J., *Tales of the Field: On Writing Ethnography* (Chicago, IL: University of Chicago Press, 1988).

Witherell, C., & Noddings, N. *Stories Lives Tell: Narrative and Dialogue in Education* (New York: Teachers' College Press, 1991).

Wolcott, H., *Writing up Qualitative Research* (Newbury Park: Sage, 1990).

Zeller, N., *A Rhetoric for Naturalistic Inquiry* Unpublished doctoral dissertation (Bloomington, IN: Indiana University, 1987).

Acknowledgements

My deep appreciation to these colleagues:
Ken Aigen
Margaret Anzul
Lynn Becker
Laurie Diefenbach
Carol di Tosti
Maryann Downing
Michelle Haddad
Rita Kopf
Elizabeth Merrick
Rebecca Mlynarczyk
Jill Schehr
Sharon Shelton
Judy Walenta

WHAT I WOULD LIKE TO DISCUSS WITH YOU

Jack Whitehead

In responding to your paper, **Write On: Stories About Telling It**, I recall the way you read your paper at the CARN Conference in September, 1992. You captivated the imaginations of your audience. It was a wonderful artistic performance. The applause was heartwarming. The way you read the playlets and vignettes helped us to feel Amanda's distress in **No A for Amanda** and to identify with Sharon's delightful understanding of her pupils.

You read the paper and the performance was a work of art. This isn't just my judgement. There were many similar comments from your audience. What we had experienced were the qualities of an artist creating an aesthetic sense of unity in her audience.

In responding to your paper I want to explore a vague intuition that the brightness and focus of your passionate intensity needs to bend a little in order to illuminate further the value of story for action researchers who are trying to improve their practice and to present an authentic account of their work in a way which clarifies their values through their emergence in practice.

I want to suggest that you have concentrated on the rhetorical criteria of story, in the sense of persuading a reader of the believability of the account. You have created an intimate link between these criteria and the very core of how we wish to represent ourselves. You invite us to improve the quality of our stories by asking such questions as:

> *Is what I am writing clear? Does it avoid the overblown? Am I inviting my readers in close or am I setting a barrier? How do I use natural language? Does it avoid generalization? How does it give voice to the people I studied? to me? Generally, is my report reader-friendly? ...* **and so we search to find a voice that is compatible with our personal vision.** (my emphasis).

I wonder if this point marks a difference between us which is related to your free interchange of the terms action, qualitative, and ethnographic research. I am reminded of Colin Henry's excellent evaluation of the First World Congress on Action Research and

Process Management. He asked researchers to ensure that they understood the fundamental principles which gave a meaning and structure to their research and which could be used to distinguish it from other forms of research which had their own defining characteristics.

You may be correct in emphasising rhetorical criteria for qualitative and ethnographic research. By underplaying dialectical criteria for action research, to the extent of a total omission in your stories about telling it, I wonder if you may have missed the heart of the matter of the **it** of your title?

What I am thinking of is the warning Kierkegaard gave of the power of art to create a unity in the imagination which served to deflect attention away from the heart of the matter. In Kierkegaard's case this was expressed in living a practical Christian life. In my own case it is related to contributing to the creation of a good social order.

By focusing on rhetorical criteria I think you encourage your readers to find a voice which is compatible with their personal vision. I think the way the vision is expressed creates a unity in our imaginations which has the power to evoke a range of emotional responses. Our feelings are aroused and the art of the presentation has enabled us to see in a new way.

Let me return to dialectics and try to explain why action researchers need a refocusing of your talents to help them understand further the value of story. The nucleus of dialectics is contradiction. The conflict between formal logicians and dialecticians has a 2000 year history. I think Plato put it well when he said that we have two ways in which we come to know. We break things down into separate components and we bring things together under a general idea. As Socrates says, the art of the dialectician is in holding both the many and the one together. When Aristotle, in his work on Interpretation, claimed that two mutually exclusive statements couldn't be true simultaneously, and that a questioner had to decide whether a person had a characteristic or not, he set the guidelines for the elimination of contradictions from theory.

I want to show how the rhetorical criteria you use may be masking a story of the power of action research to improve the quality of practice. As I write I am becoming clearer about that vague intuition I started with. I feel some awkwardness in being critical of a presentation I enjoyed so much, but on reflection I think the power of your rhetoric is masking a dialectical truth and the value of story for action researchers. I think the masking is unintentional and may be linked to a limited understanding of the nature of action research. I think this limitation can be seen in your recognition that the hallmark of many action researchers is that ***they study aspects of their own situation and apply some of their insights or hunches in ongoing rounds - that great continuous recursive tango.***

For me the hallmark of action researchers is that they are studying themselves as they attempt to improve the quality of their practice, their understanding of their practice and the social context in which the practice is located.

In other words, questions of the kind, 'How do I improve ...?' characterise the dominant action research communities. Now, once the action researcher begins to engage with her question and to produce an account, I do agree that all the rhetorical approaches you provide might help her to provide not just a believable account but one which can withstand a number of tests of validity. For example, we might ask whether or not the evidence presented in the story is sufficient to justify the claim being made. We might ask if the meaning of the values which form part of any educational enquiry are clearly shown emerging in practice and are justified in relation to a personal and/or social context. We can ask if the story is authentic in the sense that the action researcher shows over time that he or she is truly committed to the values revealed in the account. Where the sense of dialectic from an action research perspective, when an individual is answering questions of the kind, 'How do I improve ... ?', is missing from your paper can be seen in the omission of any examples which present the evidence to show what any pupil has learnt with any teacher. In my experience of teachers' action research the focus of classroom enquiry does involve pupils' learning. We have examples of teachers' stories which include detailed evidence on pupils' learning, judgements on its quality, and examples of the validation groups which subject the teachers' stories to rigorous analysis in relation to the criteria above.

In these stories the teachers acknowledge the existence of their own 'I's' as living contradictions in their practice. This is the nucleus of their dialectical accounts. They use some of the rhetorical criteria you illustrate, but as action researchers they test the validity of their rhetoric within a dialectical process.

I have now come to a precise understanding of my unease with your paper. I think its rhetoric masks a dialectical truth about the stories of the action researchers in the educational community I belong to. I think the masking becomes evident in your use of the rhetorical device 'I, Margot'. You use your paper to display an impressive range of understanding of rhetoric. The 'I, Margot' in the presentation appealed to your audience as a beautiful and good human being. At no point do you reveal 'I, Margot' as a living contradiction, located within a particular social context in which fundamental values are negated, and asking questions of the kind, 'How do I improve ...?'

It may well be that you feel no interest in asking such a question or in presenting your own story of your answers. However, in your free interplay between action, qualitative and ethnographic research, you may have missed an essential feature of action research in the nucleus of dialectics which is contradiction. On the basis of experiencing a concern, for example, because they experience the denial of their values, action researchers often imagine ways of improving their practice. They decide on an action plan, act, gather evidence and evaluate the effectiveness of their actions. They often modify their initial concern or problem, their ideas and their actions in the light of their evaluations.

At no point in your paper did I get a sense of story which included this common-sense yet disciplined form of action enquiry. We have examples of Higher Degrees at the University of Bath where the stories of the action researchers include such action reflection cycles, sometimes in the dialectical form of question and answer, and always containing some acknowledgement of the experience of themselves as living contradictions. They also show the meaning of their values emerging in practice. They are also alert to the importance of captivating the imaginations of their readers and pay some attention to the aesthetic qualities of their presentations.

From my reading of qualitative and ethnographic research I can appreciate that these researchers do not study their own learning through answering questions of the kind, 'How do I improve my practice?' or 'How do I live my values more fully in my practice?' I would imagine that these researchers would identify with the rhetorical criteria in your paper.

However, in your paper on ***Stories About Telling It***, I wonder if the **its** in qualitative, ethnographic and action research should be clearly distinguished, so that we can appreciate better the value of your stories and rhetoric for the different research traditions, and, in particular, for action research, because the paper was addressed to an International Conference of the Collaborative Action Research Network.

I have tried to point towards a number of characteristics of action research, in particular its dialectical character, which usefully and validly could be reflected back to a reader in the story. I am thinking of stories which are not only believable in the rhetorical sense that they persuade, but stories which can also withstand some rigorous tests in the dialectic of question and answer. Perhaps 'I, Margot' and 'I, Jack' should offer stories of our educational development, as part of the process of accountability in which we are concerned, about the extent to which we have contributed to the creation of a good social order and to the quality of education of the students in our care.

AND IN REPLY

Margot Ely

1a.   **REACTION ONE**
    Yes!
    Yes, of course!
    Right!

1b.   **REACTION TWO**
    Yes!
    Yes, of course!
    Right!
    Then again -
        Maybe.
        Maybe not.
    Actually -
        No.
    No! I think not.

2.   **VIGNETTE**

When I, Margot, was four and a half, I lived an event of unparalleled importance. I, the one who had chafed at the waiting, I was going to begin school. I was ecstatic. I primped and polished and practised. I drove my parents to enact creative but futile strategies to calm me down. I slept fitfully and my bathroom habits took turns for the worse. I was a mess. I was glorious.

On THE day, I set off with my new shoes, my new dress, my new bag with new pencils. I was finally at heaven's gates. It was all going to become clear now.

The first morning began. After a long time, I felt troubled. A bit more time, and I felt seriously depressed. Something was not right. Something was absolutely wrong. I tried to stifle my sobs, but they became slurpier and louder and more alarming, even to me. 'What is the matter, darling?' asked Aunt Erna, the warm and caring teacher, as she bent down to embrace my shaking and shattered self. 'Are you hurt? Are you ill?' 'No,' I managed to gasp out, 'but I've been here such a long time now and I haven't even learned to read the books! I haven't even learned to write a letter! I haven't even done my numbers!'

Aunt Erna nodded. She thought a while and then said, 'Margot, you've been here just a little bit, even though it seems so long to you. Just an hour. You can't do everything, all at once, in one hour.'

3.   A VIS-A-VIS INTERVIEW

M1 Now Margot, why in the world did you decide to focus on rhetorical criteria in your speech when you knew there were others?

M2 Good question. It is true that I was aware of many other criteria for the writing of research reports. Lincoln and Guba (1990) present four groupings of criteria for judging the quality of case study reports that I consider useful. Rhetorical criteria became the focus of my presentation. Criteria of resonance help us to assess the degree of congruence between what is written, how it is written and the belief system that powers the particular paradigm the researcher has followed. Applicability criteria help people to judge what of the report may be applicable to their own situations. Criteria of empowerment, Lincoln and Guba's fourth and final grouping, are those that speak to how the report facilitates action on the part of the readers in situations where they judge action is warranted.

With my usual appetite, I really planned to talk about all four groups of criteria. I began by fleshing out each category with examples from the field. It didn't take me too long to understand that while I could skate hastily over all, bringing even one category to life was a formidable task within the time limits. At that point, I decided to focus on rhetorical criteria. I felt, and still do, that they are not highlighted sufficiently for budding or seasoned researchers, even though the writing of a research report or paper is often a tremendous sticking point. This sort of avoidance piqued my interest because, after all, our rhetoric is the medium for our message. I hesitated some, however. I am not an 'English Educator'. I am not expert in the field of writing, and I half feared the rolling eyes of some of my colleagues who are such experts. Nevertheless!

Next, my decision about focus was urged by my support group. This time around it was in the persons of Margaret Anzul and Maryann Downing, who, being privy to my first run-through, which left them glassy eyed, literally insisted that I stay with one area as deeply as I could. And last, there were the words of Aunt Erna.

M1 Why were you asked to present a keynote at CARN?

M2 Tony read my book when it was first published, wrote to me about it, and we began a correspondence - of sorts. That was the fatal beginning. About a year later the planning committee people asked me to speak, with the understanding that I use the umbrella term 'qualitative researcher' and that I work to make the issue of rhetorical criteria compatible and meaningful to the action researchers at CARN.

M1 Why did you make the point that all the people who provided vignettes and examples for the speech were action researchers?

M2 Each person was a doctoral student, a graduate immersed in fieldwork and in learning the craft of the research. Each contribution was related to the recursive process of personal learning, of improving as a researcher. Thus, in my way of viewing the world, we were all action researchers. No matter what we were studying in the field, and no matter what we titled the paradigm, we held the above in common. What we held in common, also, was that as a group as well as with other researchers, we needed to write our reports - and that was my springboard.

Where I am somewhat at sea with the critique, however, is with the statements that the paper's vignettes had nothing to do with the question 'How do I improve?' To me, the work is peppered through with examples of people who keep asking just that. Look at Rebecca's concern with what she sees as her overcontrol in the classroom; at Judy's caution that she learn to counter her 'White Knight Syndrome'; at Carole's difficult decision to write her report in her superintendent's spirit rather than to take the easy way; at Jill's insights about how to fight her own preconceptions, both as a therapist and as a researcher. Is it that the examples seemed too far afield? Surely, it cannot be that all the examples needed to be of a particular sort of classroom life. That would truncate action research tremendously, in my opinion. Is it that I did not add further layers of what was learned, done and redone?

M1 Now, to take the bull by the horns. What is your stance on the similarities and differences between and among types of alternative paradigms such as ethnographic, heuristic, action research?

M2 Oh, No! You can't trick me like that! This subject demands a great deal more time, thought and space than I can give. However, I feel like beginning, even though I think I hear the screams reverberating in the hallowed halls even as I compose this.

At this point, I suspect that far more binds together that great middle-of-the-pack group of 'sorts' of field-based qualitative research described by Tesch than separates them. I am less certain than Colin Henry is described to be that there are indeed all these clear, crisp, distinguishing characteristics that delineate each single research paradigm. For example, while Jack describes it as the hallmark of action researchers, I know of no qualitative field researchers of any ilk who do not seek to study themselves 'as they attempt to improve the quality of their practice, their understanding of their practice and the social context in which the practice is located'. Further, I know of no qualitative field researcher of any ilk who does not use, indeed who does not celebrate, contradiction as a spur, especially when this contradiction signals a denial of personal values.

But I did not go to Worcester to discuss the case for similarities and differences across alternative paradigms. My presentation was built, on purpose, to embrace a larger number of forms of research because I feel it serves action researchers to see what some of their colleague-cousins are doing and learning; to reach for a wider view of action research - and here I am in agreement with Ken Zeichner's call for a more extended vision of social betterment and social activism by action researchers (Zeichner, 1992); and to talk of report writing issues that touch all of us.

M1 What is the difference between your description of the hallmark of many action researchers:

They study aspects of their own situations and apply some of their insights or hunches in ongoing rounds - that great continuous recursive tango

and Jack's description of the hallmarks?

They are studying themselves as they attempt to improve the quality of their practice, their understanding of their practice and the social context in which the practice is located.

M2 I see no essential difference. Certainly, the words are different. My version assumes the audience to understand that action researchers are part of the very situations they study and that applying insights and hunches in rounds has to do with both improving and deepening understanding. Jack's version is more public about that. My version is more public about painting a picture of the core process - 'that great continuous recursive tango'.

M1 How do you feel about Jack's critique as a whole?

M2 Beautifully written. Strong. Pulls no punches. I knew when I attended Jack's workshop that I'd like to count him as a colleague - to work with him, fight with him, fight 'systems' with him. I'm more convinced of that now.

Jack's critique is telling to me in another way. In its drive, its momentum, it combines into a particularly masculinist tapestry, one that rather neatly sets up a Straw Woman of me as author-presenter. In it, I am charming, rather superficial, manipulative - albeit unintentionally so - , limited in scope and understanding of action research, misusing art to deflect people's attention away from what really counts, not given to self-disclosure as 'a living contradiction located with a particular social context in which fundamental values are negated', not given to asking the difficult questions, such as 'How can I improve?'; 'How can I better live my values?'

Not a very nice picture, but one that can be used as a template by my readers as they return once again to look at ***Write On: Stories About Telling It.***

References

Zeichner, K., 'Action Research: Personal Renewal and Social Reconstruction': a Paper presented at the International Conference of the Collaborative Action Research Network, Worcester College of Higher Education, UK (September, 1992).

Bibliography

Altrichter, H., Posch, P., and Somekh, B., *Teachers Investigate Their Work* (Routledge, 1993).

Atkinson, P., *Understanding Ethnographic Text* (Newbury Park, CA: Sage, 1992).

Berthoff, A., *The Making of Meaning* (Boynton Cook, New Jersey, 1981).

Beyer, L., 'What knowledge is of most worth in teacher education?' in Smyth, J., *Educating Teachers: Changing the Nature of Pedagogical Knowledge* (Falmer Press, Sussex, 1987).

Brownhill, R.J., *Education and the Nature of Knowledge* (Croom Helm, 1983).

Burton, J., *Languages Inservice Program for Teachers: Stage 1, 1988 - A Pilot Project (External Evlauation).* (SA Education Department, 1989).

Burton, J., *Languages Inservice Program for Teachers: LIPT 2 Evaluation - Discussion Paper (LIPT Training Practice and the Resulting Professional Renewal)* (Adelaide: SA Education Department, 1990).

Burton, J., *LIPT: Where Next? Aims and Achievements from LIPT 1 to LIPT 3 (A Case Study Evaluation of LIPT 3 with Reference to the Evaluations of LIPTs 1 and 2).* (Adelaide: SA Education Department, 1991).

Burton, J., *The Languages Inservice Program for Teachers of Language other than English, 1988-1991).* (Adelaide: SA Education Department, 1992).

Burton, J. and Mickan, P., 'Teachers' classroom research: rhetoric and reality' in Edge, J. and Richards, K. (eds.), *Teachers Develop, Teachers Research* (Heinemann, 1993).

Cameron, D., Frazer, E., Harvey, P., Rampton, M.B.H., and Richardson, K., *Researching Language: Issues of Power and Method* (London: Routledge, 1992).

Carr, W. and Kemmis, S., *Becoming Critical: Knowing Through Action Research* (Geelong: Deakin University Press, 1983).

Carroll, J. and Manne, R. (eds.), *Shutdown: The Failure of Economic Rationalism and How to Rescue Australia* (Melbourne: Text Publishing Company, 1992).

Collier, J., 'United States Indian Administration as a laboratory of ethnic affairs' in Social Research, 12 (1945).

Collingwood, R.G., *Speculum Mentis, or The Map of Knowledge* (Clarendon Press, Oxford, 1924).

Comey, D.D., 'Logic' in Kernig *Marxism, Communism and Western Society* (Harder and Harder, New York, 1972).

Corey, S.M., 'Action research, fundamental research and educational practices' in Teachers' College Record, Vol. 50 (May, 1949). Reprinted in Kemmis, S. and McTaggart, R. (eds.), *The Action Research Reader* (Geelong: Deakin University Press, 1988).

Corey, S.M., *Action Research to Improve School Practices* (New York, Teachers' College, Columbia University, 1953).

Department of Employment, Education and Training (DEET), Teachers

Learning (Canberra: Australian Government Publishing Service (AGPS), 1988).

Dewey, J., *The Child and the Curriculum; The School and Society* (Chicago; The University of Chicago Press, 1902).

Dunlop, R., *Professional Development. A Review of Contemporary Literature* mimeo (Queensland, Australia: Department of Education, 1990).

Eames, K., *The Growth of a Teacher-Researcher's Attempt to Understand Writing, Redrafting, Learning and Autonomy in the Examination Years* (MPhil Dissertation, University of Bath, 1987).

Eames, K., 'Dialogues and Dialectics': a Paper presented at the International Conference of the Collaborative Action Research Network, University of East Anglia (1989a); later published in Edwards, G. and Rideout, P. (eds.), *Extending the Horizons of Action Research* (CARN Publication 10C, 1991).

Eames, K., *Personal Growth through Students Reviewing their own Writing* (Bassett Action Research Group, Wootton Bassett School, Swindon, Wiltshire, 1989b).

Eames, K., (ed.) *How can we Improve Professionalism in Education Through Collaborative Action Research?* (Bassett Action Research Group, Wootton Bassett School, Swindon, Wiltshire, 1989c).

Eames, K., 'Growing your own' in British Journal of In-Service Education, Vol. 16, No. 2 (Autumn, 1990). Reprinted in McNiff, J., *Teaching as Learning: an Action Research Approach* (Routledge, London and New York, 1993).

Elliott, J., 'Developing hypotheses about classrooms from teachers' practical constructs: an account of the Ford Teaching Project': a Paper presented at the Annual Meeting, American Educational Research Association, San Francisco, California (April, 1976).

Elliott, J., 'What is action research?': a Paper presented at the CARN Conference, Wolfson Court, Cambridge (7-9 July, 1978).

Elliott, J., 'Facilitating action research in schools: some dilemmas' in Burgess, R. (ed.), *Field Methods in the Study of Education* (London: Falmer Press, 1985).

Elliott, J., 'What is action research in schools?' in Journal of Curriculum Studies, 10/4 (1978). Reprinted in Kemmis, S. and McTaggart, R. (eds.), *The Action Research Reader* (Geelong: Deakin University Press, 1988).

Elliott, J., 'Educational theory, practical philosophy and action research' in British Journal of Educational Studies, 35(2) (1987).

Elliott, J., 'Educational theory and the professional learning of teachers: an overview' in Cambridge Journal of Education, Vol. 19, No. 1 (1989).

Ely, M., Anzul, M., Friedman, T., Garner, D., and McCormack, A., *Doing Qualitative Research: Circles Within Circles* (London and New York, Falmer, 1991).

Engels, F., *Dialectics of Nature* (Progress Publishers, Moscow, 1934).

Fals Borda, O., 'Investigating reality in order to transform it: The Colombian Experience' in Dialectical Anthropology, IV/I (March, 1979). Reprinted in Kemmis, S. and McTaggart, R. (eds.), *The Action Research Reader* (Geelong: Deakin University Press, 1988).

Fals Borda, O., 'The application of participatory action research in Latin America' in International Sociology, II/4 (December, 1987).

Fals Borda, O., *Knowledge and People's Power: Lessons with the Peasants in Nicaragua, Mexico and Colombia* (New York: New Horizons Press, 1988).

Fals Borda, O., 'Evolution and convergences in participatory action research': a Paper presented at the Participatory Research Conference, 'A Celebration of People's Knowledge', University of Calgary, Calgary, July, 1989 (Calgary: The Division of International Development, The International Centre, University of Calgary, 1989).

Fals Borda, O., 'Investigating reality in order to change it: a conversation with Orlando Fals Borda and Stephen Kemmis': videorecording made during the Participatory Research Conference, 'A Celebration of People's Knowledge', University of Calgary, Calgary, July, 1989). (Calgary: The Division of International Development, The International Centre, University of Calgary, 1989).

Fals Borda, O. and Rahman Mohammed, A., *Action and Knowledge* (New York: The Apex Press, 1991).

Fals Borda, O. (forthcoming), 'Contexts and consequences of participatory action research in Colombia: some personal feelings': Chapter in McTaggart, R. (forthcoming), *Participatory Research: Contexts and Consequences* (no other details).

Foucault, M., *Power/Knowledge* (Harvester Press, Sussex, 1975).

Freeman, D., 'Language teacher education, emerging discourse, and change in classroom practice' in Flowerdew, J., Brock, M., and Hsia, S., *Perspectives on Second Language Teacher Education* (Hong Kong: City Polytechnic of Hong Kong, 1992).

Fullan, M., *What's Worth Fighting For in the Principalship?* (Melbourne:Council for Educational Leadership, 1991).

Gadamer, H.G., *Truth and Method* (New York, Seabury Press, 1975).

Gaventa, J., 'The powerful, the powerless and the experts: knowledge in an information age: draft for Chapter in Part, P., Hall, B., and Jackson, T. (eds.), *Participatory Research in America* (no other details).

Grundy, S. and Kemmis, S., 'Educational action research in Australia: the state of the art (an overview)', in Kemmis, S. and McTaggart, S. (eds.), *The Action Research Reader* (Geelong: Deakin University Press, 1988).

Guba, E. and Lincoln, Y., *Fourth Generation Evaluation* (Newbury Park, CA: Sage, 1989).

Hamilton, D., 'The pedagogical juggernaut' in British Journal of Educational Studies, 35 (1986).

Hardy, B., 'Narrative as a primary act of the mind', in Meek, M., Warlow, A.

and Barton, G. (eds.), *The Cool Web: Patterns of Children's Reading* (New York: Atheneum, 1978).
Henry, C. and Edwards, B., 'Enduring a lot: the effects of the school system on students with non-English-speaking backgrounds'. Human Rights Commission Education Series, no. 3 (Canberra: Australian Government Printing Services, 1986).
Henry. C., 'If action research were tennis': Chapter 9 in Zuber-Skerritt, O. (ed.), *Action Learning for Improved Performance* (Brisbane: AEBIS Publishing, 1991).
Hirst, P.H., 'Educational theory' in Tibble, J.W. (ed.), *The Study of Education* (London, Routledge and Kegan Paul, 1966).
Hirst, P.H., 'Educational theory' in Hirst, P.H., *Educational Theory and Its Foundation Disciplines* (London, Routledge and Kegan Paul, 1983).
Horne, D., 'Australia: time for a rethink' (The Age, Melbourne. 1992).
Horne, D. (ed.), *The Trouble with Economic Rationalism* (Melbourne: Scribe Publications, 1992).
Ilyenkov, E.V., *Dialectical Logic* (Moscow, Progress Publishers, 1977).
Kemmis, S., 'Critical educational research': a Paper prepared for the Critical Theory Pre-conference of the North American Adult Education Association Research Conference, University of Calgary, Calgary (1988).
Kemmis, S., 'Postmodernism and educational research': a Paper prepared for the seminar 'Methodology and Epistemology in Educational Research' sponsored by the Economic and Social Research Council: Department of Education, University of Liverpool (1992).
Kemmis, S. and McTaggart, R. (eds.) *The Action Research Reader* (Geelong: Deakin University Press, 1988).
Kemmis, S. and McTaggart, R., *The Action Research Planner* (Geelong: Deakin University Press, 1988).
Klafki, W., 'Decentralised curriculum development in the form of action research' in Council of Europe Research Bulletin, No. 1 (1975). Reprinted in Kemmis, S. and McTaggart, R. (eds.), *The Action Research Reader* (Geelong: Deakin University Press, 1988).
Laidlaw, M., *Action Research: A Guide for Use on Second Teaching Practice* (mimeographed handbook, University of Bath, 1991).
Larter, A.P., *An Action-Research Approach to Classroom Discussion in the Examination Years* (MPhil Dissertation, University of Bath, 1987).
Lawlor, S., *Teachers Mistaught - Training in Theories of Education in Subjects* (Centre for Policy Studies, 1990).
Lewin, K., *Field Theory in Social Science* (New York; Harper and Row, 1951).
Lincoln, Y. and Guba, E., 'Judging the quality of case study reports' in International Journal of Qualitative Studies in Education, 0951-8398/90 (1990).
Manne, R., 'The cruel experiment' in The Age Extra, Melbourne (29 August, 1992).
McCullough, D., in *The New York Times* (August, 1992).

McIntyre, A., *After Virtue: A Study in Moral Theory* (London: Duckworth, 1988).
McNiff, J., *Action Research: Principles and Practice* (Macmillan Education, 1988: Routledge, London and New York, 1992).
McNiff, J., Whitehead, J., and Laidlaw, M., and Members of the Bath Action Research Group, *Creating A Good Social Order Through Action Research* (Hyde Publications, 1992).
McTaggart, R., 'Pedagogical principles for Aboriginal teacher education' in The Aboriginal Child at School, 15/4 (1987).
McTaggart, R., 'Aboriginalisation involves empowerment and disempowerment' in The Aboriginal Child at School, 17/2 (1987).
McTaggart, R., 'Reductionism and action research: technology versus convivial forms of life': Keynote address presented at the Second World Congress on Action Learning, University of Queensland, Brisbane (1992).
Nias, J., 'Teaching and the self' in Holly, M.L. and McLoughlin, C.S. (eds.), *Perspectives on Teacher Professional Development* (London: Falmer Press, 1989).
Nixon, J. (ed.), *A Teacher's Handbook to Action Research* (London: Grant McIntyre, 1981).
Oja, S. and Smulyan, L., *Collaborative Action Research: A Developmental Approach* (London: Falmer Press, 1989).
Paley, V.G., 'You can't say you can't play: Free choice, friendship, and fairness among young children': Address delivered at the Eleventh International Human Science Research Conference, Rochester, Oakland University (1992).
Papert, S., *Mindstorms: Children, Computers and Powerful Ideas* (Harvester Press, 1980).
Peters, R.S., 'What is an educational process?' in Peters, R.S. (ed.), *The Concept of Education* (London, Routledge and Kegan Paul, 1967).
Pettman, R., *Teaching for Human Rights* (Melbourne: Hodja, 1984).
Pitken, H. and Shumer, M., 'On participation' in Democracy, Vol. 2 (Fall, 1982).
Plato, *Phaedrus* (trans. Hamilton, W., London, Penguin, 1973).
Polanyi, M., *Personal Knowledge: Towards a Post-Critical Philosophy* (Routledge and Kegan Paul, 1958).
Research Intelligence: Newsletter of the British Educational Research Association (No. 37, 1990).
Richards, C., 'Management development through action learning in Australia Post': a Chapter in Zuber-Skerritt, O. (ed.), *Action Learning for Improved Performance* (Brisbane: AEBIS Publishing, 1991).
Rizvi, F., *Williams on Democracy and the Governance of Education* Mimeo (Geelong: Deakin University School of Education, 1989).
Rushdie, S., in *The New York Times* (December, 1991).
Schön, D., *The Reflective Practitioner* (Basic Books, New York, 1983).
Shor, I., *Critical Teaching and Everyday Life* (Boston: South End Press, 1980).

Shumsky, A., 'Co-operation in action research: a rationale' in Journal of Educational Sociology, Vol. 30 (1956). Reprinted in Kemmis, S. and McTaggart, R. (eds.), *The Action Research Reader* (Geelong: Deakin University Press, 1988).

Somekh, B., 'Pupil Autonomy in Learning with Microcomputers: rhetoric or reality? An action research study' in Cambridge Journal of Education, Vol. 21, No. 1 (1991).

Sonnichsen, R., 'Advocacy evaluation: a model for internal evaluation offices' in Evaluation and Program Planning, Vol. 11 (1988).

Stenhouse, L., *An Introduction to Curriculum Research and Development* (London: Heinemann, 1975).

Strauss, A., *Qualitative Analysis for Social Scientists* (Cambridge, Cambridge University Press, 1987).

Tax, S., 'Action anthropology' in Gearing, F., Netting, R., and Peattie, L. (eds.), *Documentary of the FOX Project, 1948-1959: Program of action anthropology* (Chicago: University of Chicago, 1960). Reprinted in Kemmis, S. and McTaggart, R. (eds.), *The Action Research Reader* (Geelong: Deakin University Press, 1988).

The Times Educational Supplement (6th September, 1990).

The Times Educational Supplement (22nd March, 1991).

Tyler, S.A., *The Unspeakable: Discourse, Dialogue, and Rhetoric in the Postmodern World* (Madison, WI: University of Wisconsin Press, 1987).

Van Maanen, J., *Tales of the Field: On Writing Ethnography* (Chicago, IL: University of Chicago Press, 1988).

Van Manen, M., 'Reflectivity and the pedagogical moment: the normativity of pedagogical thinking and acting' in Journal of Curriculum Studies, 23/6 (1991).

Weiner, G., 'Professional self knowledge versus social justice: a critical analysis of the teacher researcher movement' in British Educational Research Journal, Vol. 15 (1989).

Williams, R., *Towards 2000* (London: Chatto and Windus, 1983).

Winter, R., *Learning From Experience: Principles and Practice in Action Research* (London: The Falmer Press, 1989).

Witherell, C. and Noddings, N., *Stories Lives Tell: Narrative and Dialogue in Education* (New York: Teachers' College Press, 1991).

Wolcott, H., *Writing Up Qualitative Research* (Newbury Park: Sage, 1990).

Zeichner, K., *Connecting Genuine Teacher Development to the Struggle for Social Justice* mimeo (University of Wisconsin, Madison, 1991).

Zeichner, K., 'Action research: personal renewal and social reconstruction': a Paper presented at the International Conference of the Collaborative Action Research Network, Worcester College of Higher Education, UK (September, 1992).

Zeller, N., *A Rhetoric for Naturalistic Inquiry* Unpublished doctoral dissertation (Bloomington, IN: Indiana State University, 1987).

Index

action research
  cycles 3, 10, 11, 14, 20, 28, 33, 36, 108, 130
  its holistic nature 36, 73
  its wide applicability 28, 101
Altrichter, H. 47
appraisal of teachers 26
Atkinson, P. 107, 110, 115, 127

Bath Action Research Group 22
Bath, University of 15, 16
Berthoff, A. 8, 17
Beyer, L. 12, 17
Botham, I. 62, 77
British Educational Research Association (BERA) 26
Brownhill, R.J. 12, 17
Bruner, J. 110
Burton, J. 83-4, 87-8, 93, 96-7, 102-3

Cameron, D. et al 95, 97
Carr, W. 58-9, 70, 75, 78, 97
Clay, N. 1, 19
clinical teaching in anaesthesia 28-36
collaborative action research (see also participatory action research) 1, 58, 100
Collaborative Action Research Network (CARN) 19, 47, 75, 101, 128, 132, 134
collective antonomy xi, 48, 50, 51, 73, 74, 78
Collier, J. 51, 70
Collingwood, R.G. 4, 5, 17
Comey, D.D. 5, 6, 11, 17
complexity xi, 4, 7, 11, 13, 36, 112
conflicting values 69
contradiction 5, 6, 11, 13, 14, 20, 73, 95, 130, 136
conversational forms x - xiii
Corey, S. 28, 57, 70
cyclic nature of action research - see action research cycles

d'Arcy, P. 1, 15
Deakin University xi, 47, 58, 62, 75, 76, 79
De Cet, D. 13
democratic forms ix, 44, 48, 49, 50, 74
democratisation through action research 51-2, 54, 58
Department of Employment and Training 85, 97
Dewey, J. 38-40, 43, 44
dialectical forms xi, 2, 6, 7, 9, 10, 12, 19
dialectical knowledge 4, 6, 7
dialogical forms 19, 23
dialogue 4-6, 10, 19, 24-5
dialogue of equals ix, 23-5, 61, 79, 92
Dunlop, R. 85, 86, 97

Eames, K. 1, 2, 7, 14-17, 23
East Anglia, University of 47
educational knowledge xi, xii, 1-3, 5-7, 9-12, 14, 21
educational theory 2, 38, 59
Edwards, B. 58, 71
Elliott, J. 3, 7, 18, 21, 28, 30, 36, 38, 57, 70, 86, 97
Ely, M. 105-127, 133-137
Engels, F. 6, 18
ethnographic research 109, 112, 123, 129, 132
evolving forms ix, 4, 5, 9, 24, 114

Fals Borda, O. 52-6, 63, 70, 75-6, 79
feelings, role of x, 1, 20
Foucault, M. 12, 18
Freeman, D. 93, 94, 97
Freire, P. viii, xii, xiii
Fullan, M. 48
funded research 103

Gadamer, H.G. 5, 18
Gaventa, J. 51-2, 71
gender issues (see also women's entitlement) 111, 137
General Teaching Council 17, 26
Ghaye, T. xiii, 134
Greendown School, Swindon 13, 16
grounded enquiry ix, 37, 59
Grundy, S. 86, 95, 97, 101
Guba, E. 106-8, 127, 134

Hamilton, D. 64, 71
Henry, C. 47-64, 71, 79-82, 129, 136
Hirst, P. 2-4, 7, 12, 13, 16-19
Horne, D. 49, 71
Horton, M. 51
human rights 63-70

Ilyenkov, E.V. 5, 6, 11
improvement through education 2, 39, 64
improving the quality of education through action research 59, 75, 79, 86, 129, 130
improving social relations 49, 50
INTENT Project 47
Kemmis, S. 58, 59, 71, 75, 78, 86, 95, 97, 101
Klafki, W. 57, 72

Laidlaw, M. 16, 18, 22
language, different forms xii, 24, 110
Languages Inservice Program for Teachers (LIPT) 83, 85, 88-92, 94-96, 98-100, 103
Larter, A. 13, 15, 18, 20
Lawlor, S. 16, 18
leadership, different kinds of 94, 95

Lehane, T. 27, 41-43
Lewin, K. 36
Lincoln, Y. 106-8, 127, 134
living contradictions 5, 11, 131
logic, forms of 2, 5, 7

management in action research 84-96
management of self xii, 85, 91, 93, 100, 102
managers, role of 86, 89, 92, 95, 96-100
Manne, R. 49, 72
McCullough, D. 112, 127
McIntyre, A. 56, 72, 81
McKernan, J. 38
McNiff, J. 3, 18, 22
McTaggart, R. 58, 61, 71-2, 75, 78, 97
Mickan, P. 83-4, 87, 102-3

narrative xii, 113, 123
networking 92, 94, 96, 99, 100
Nias, J. 93, 97
Noddings, N. 125, 127

Oja, S. 94, 95, 97, 98
'ordinary' people's knowledge 49, 51, 54, 56, 76
Otto, A. 27-45

Paley, V.G. 109
PALM Project 47, 73
Papert, S. 73, 74, 78
participatory action research (see also collaborative action research) 52, 55-6, 58, 60, 64, 75, 79
Patten, J. 43
Peattie, L. 51
personal knowledge 1, 4, 19, 25, 44, 74
personal understanding, development of 2-4, 6, 9, 15, 25
Peters, R.S. 2-4, 18
Pettman, R. 63, 72
Pitken, H. 49, 72
Plato 4, 6
Polanyi, M. 74, 78
political attack on teachers 16, 22, 43, 84
Posch, P. 47
power relationships 24-5, 50-1, 53, 57, 63
practitioners' knowledge 3, 131 (see also professional knowledge)
presenting personal accounts 20, 23, (see also report writing)
professional knowledge 1, 12, 14, 16, 26, 103
provisional nature of action research 10, 24, 25

qualitative methodologies 28, 106-128
quantitative methodologies 28-9, 36, 44, 98
question and answer 4-6, 10, 14, 132

reflection, central place of 38, 91
report writing 107, 108, 110, 112, 114, 125
researchers, full and part time 98-102
rhetorical devices 108, 109, 112, 115, 123, 129
Richards, C. 81
rigour, need for 15, 16, 21, 25, 131
Rizvi, F. 49, 72
role of teachers 39, 40
Rushdie, S. 126-7

Schön, D. 4, 9, 18, 44
school development plans 26
Scrimshaw, P. 83, 98-101
self-management (see management of self)
self, role of xi, 20, 125-6
shared understanding 3, 19, 24, 26, 60, 74, 93, 124
Shor, I. 50
Shumer, M. 49, 72
Suumsky, A. 51, 72
Smulyan, L. 94, 95, 97, 98
Social evolution through action research 51, 52, 55-7, 60
Somekh, B. 47, 73-78
Sonnichsen, R. 81
spirals 36
Stenhouse, L. 58, 72
Strauss, A. 98, 103
supporting action research 92-4, 100-1, 103

Tax, S. 51, 72
Tyler, S.A. 112, 127

values in education 44, 48, 129
value-laden activities x, 56, 57, 61
Van Maanen, J. 107, 127
Van Manen, M. 62, 72

Wakefield, P. xiv
Washington University 27
Weiner, G. 81
Whitehead, J. xiii, 15, 22, 105, 129-132
Williams, R. 49, 50, 72
Wiltshire LEA 1, 15
Winter, R. 28, 36, 38
Witherell, C. 125, 127
Wolcott, H. 107, 110, 127
women's entitlement 66-9
Worcester College of Higher Education xi, xiii, 27, 76, 137
Wootton Bassett School 1, 13-16, 26
writing, forms of xii, 20, 23, 106-126

Zeichner, K. 81, 136, 137
Zeller, N. 107, 127